WITH THE TURKISH ARMY IN THESSALY

FIELD-MARSHAL EDHEM PASHA. [*Frontispiece.*

WITH THE TURKISH ARMY IN THESSALY

BY

CLIVE BIGHAM
AUTHOR OF "A RIDE THROUGH WESTERN ASIA"

WITH ILLUSTRATIONS AND MAPS

The Naval & Military Press Ltd

published in association with

FIREPOWER
The Royal Artillery Museum
Woolwich

Published by
The Naval & Military Press Ltd
Unit 10 Ridgewood Industrial Park,
Uckfield, East Sussex,
TN22 5QE England
Tel: +44 (0) 1825 749494
Fax: +44 (0) 1825 765701
www.naval-military-press.com

in association with

FIREPOWER
The Royal Artillery Museum, Woolwich
www.firepower.org.uk

In reprinting in facsimile from the original, any imperfections are inevitably reproduced and the quality may fall short of modern type and cartographic standards.

PREFACE

This book was written directly after the conclusion of the armistice between Turkey and Greece, and before the publication of any official papers on the military operations. It only professes to be a rough sketch, and cannot lay claim to absolute accuracy of figures, though these, for the most part, are probably correct.

The writer would take this opportunity of expressing his sense of the courtesy and assistance shown him by the Imperial military and civil authorities throughout the time he spent in Turkey, and also of thanking the management of the *Times* for allowing him to make use of telegrams and letters sent by him from the seat of war and published in the columns of that journal.

C. C. B.

WHITE'S,
June 25, 1897.

CONTENTS

CHAPTER I
THE CAUSES OF THE WAR . . . . PAGE 1

CHAPTER II
THE BASE OF OPERATIONS 8

CHAPTER III
THE ARMY IN THE FIELD 16

CHAPTER IV
EDHEM PASHA AND HIS STAFF 27

CHAPTER V
THE INCURSIONS AT GREVENA AND KARYA 34

CHAPTER VI
THE BATTLE OF MILONA 42

CHAPTER VII
THE ADVANCE ON LARISSA 50

CHAPTER VIII
THE OCCUPATION OF NORTHERN THESSALY 60

CONTENTS

CHAPTER IX
THE FIRST BATTLE OF VELESTINO 66

CHAPTER X
THE ACTION OF PHARSALA 76

CHAPTER XI
THE SECOND BATTLE OF VELESTINO 83

CHAPTER XII
THE BATTLE OF DOMOKO 91

CHAPTER XIII
THE OCCUPATION OF SOUTHERN THESSALY 103

CHAPTER XIV
CONCLUSION 113

APPENDIX
SYNOPSIS OF EVENTS 129

LIST OF ILLUSTRATIONS

Field-Marshal Edhem Pasha	*Frontispiece*	
Frontier North of Meteora	*To face page*	14
Turkish Field Battery in Line	,,	22
Elassona	,,	28
Greek Advance on Karya	,,	38
Greeks below Milona	,,	46
The Battle of Mati	,,	53
Green Mosque and Bridge of Larissa	,,	61
The Battle of Velestino	,,	72
Velestino	,,	85
The Road to the South	,,	101
Turkish Field Battery in Action	,,	117

MAPS

						To face page
Position of Greek and Turkish Forces on April 1						41
,,	,,	,,	,,	,,	25	60
,,	,,	,,	,,	May	4	76
,,	,,	,,	,,	,,	10	90
,,	,,	,,	,,	,,	20	109
Map of Balkan Peninsula						*at end*

PLANS

Battle of Milona	44
First Battle of Velestino	70
Battle of Domoko	97

```
The maps and plans in this reprint are
placed after this page.
```

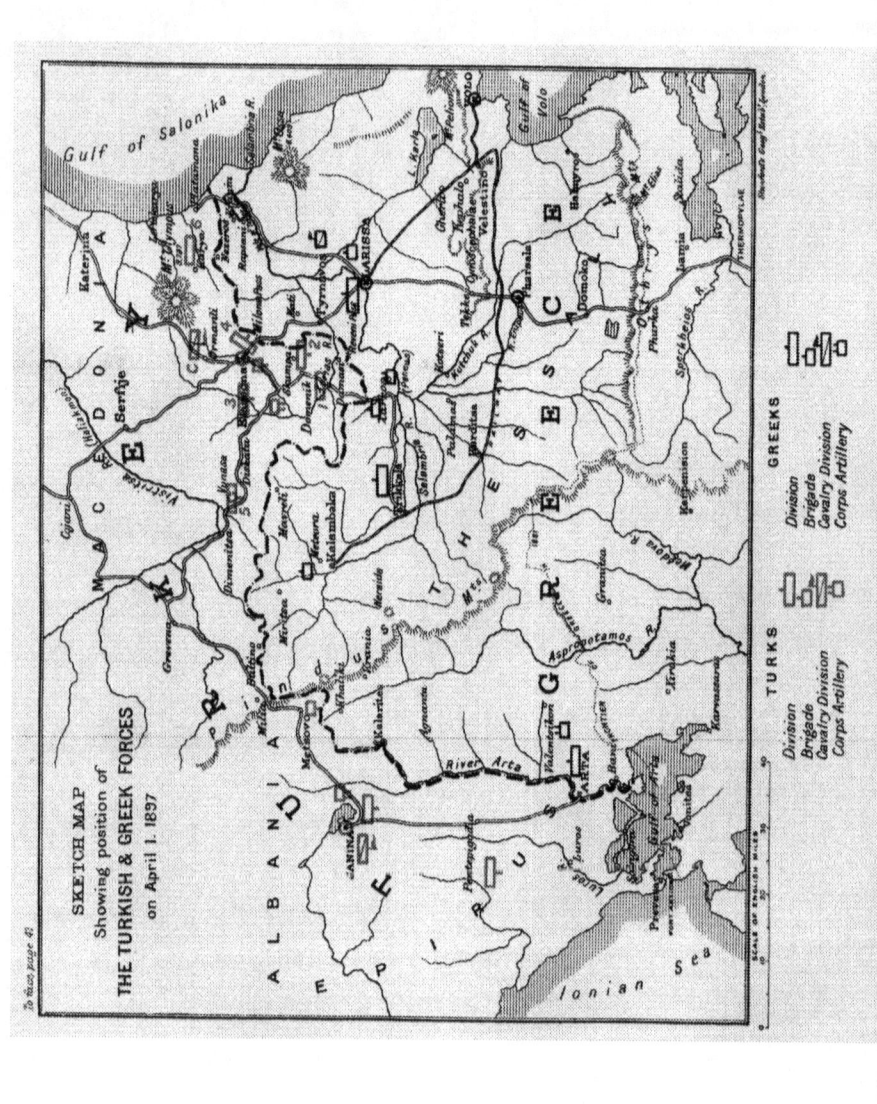

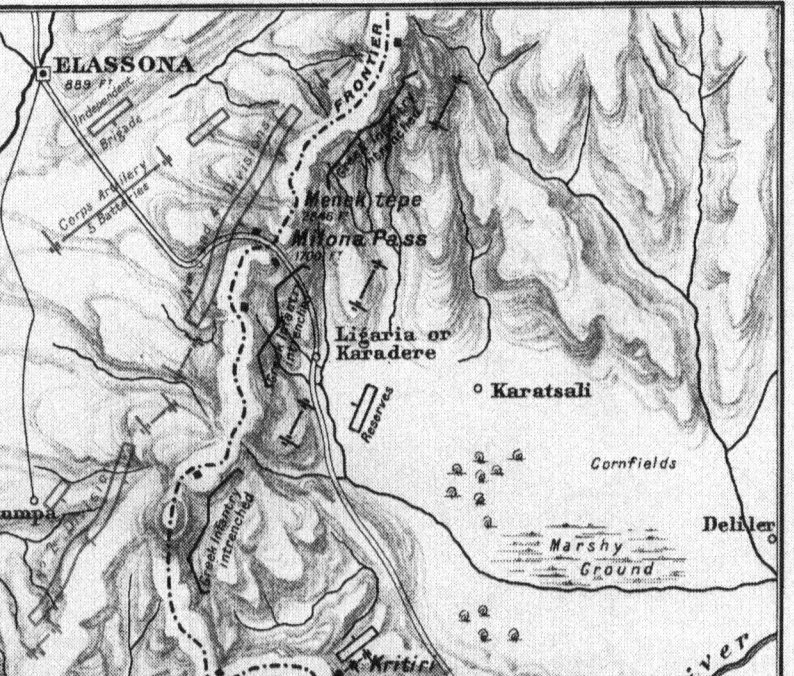

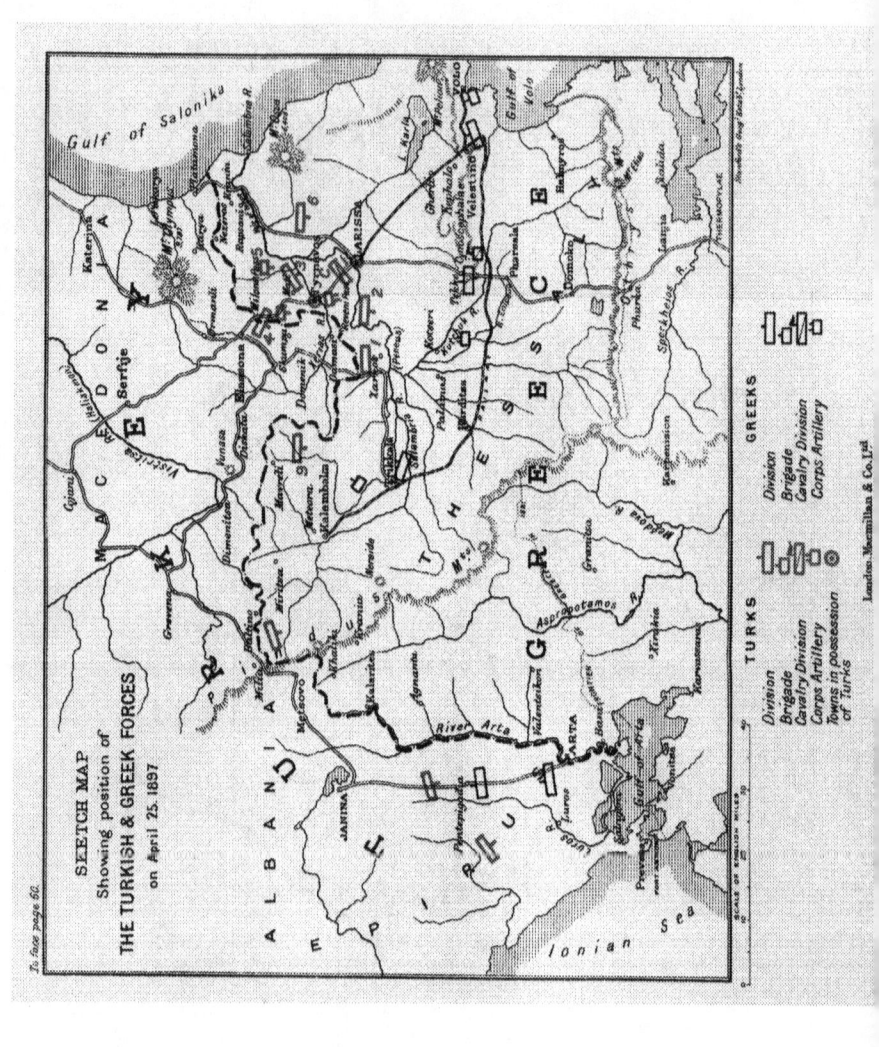

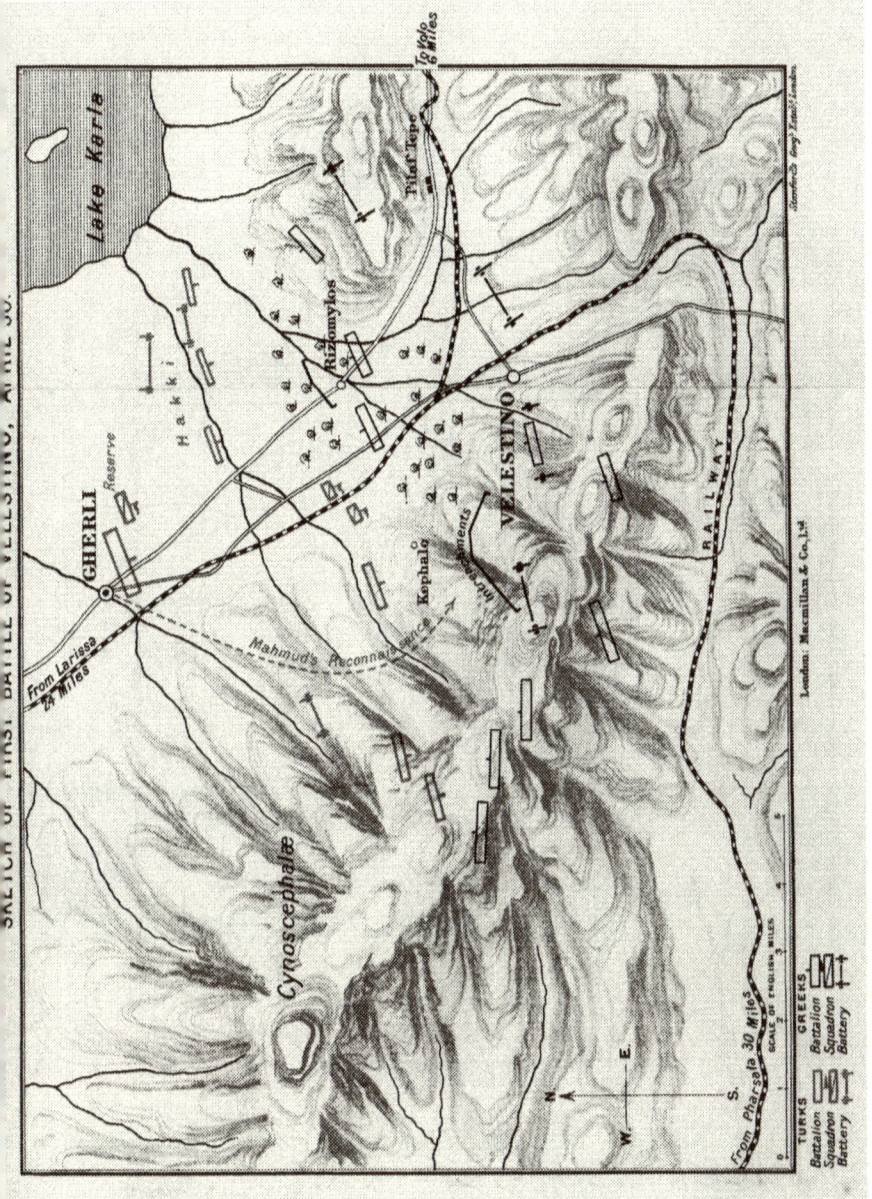

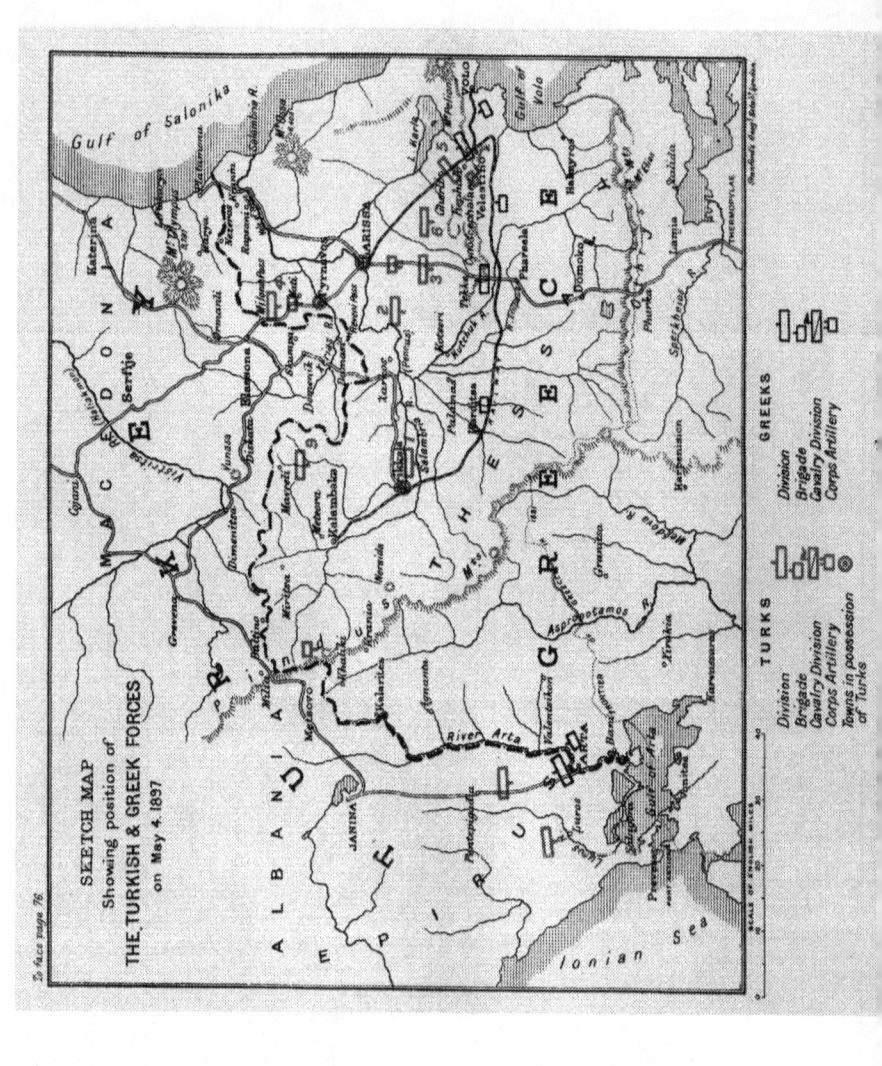

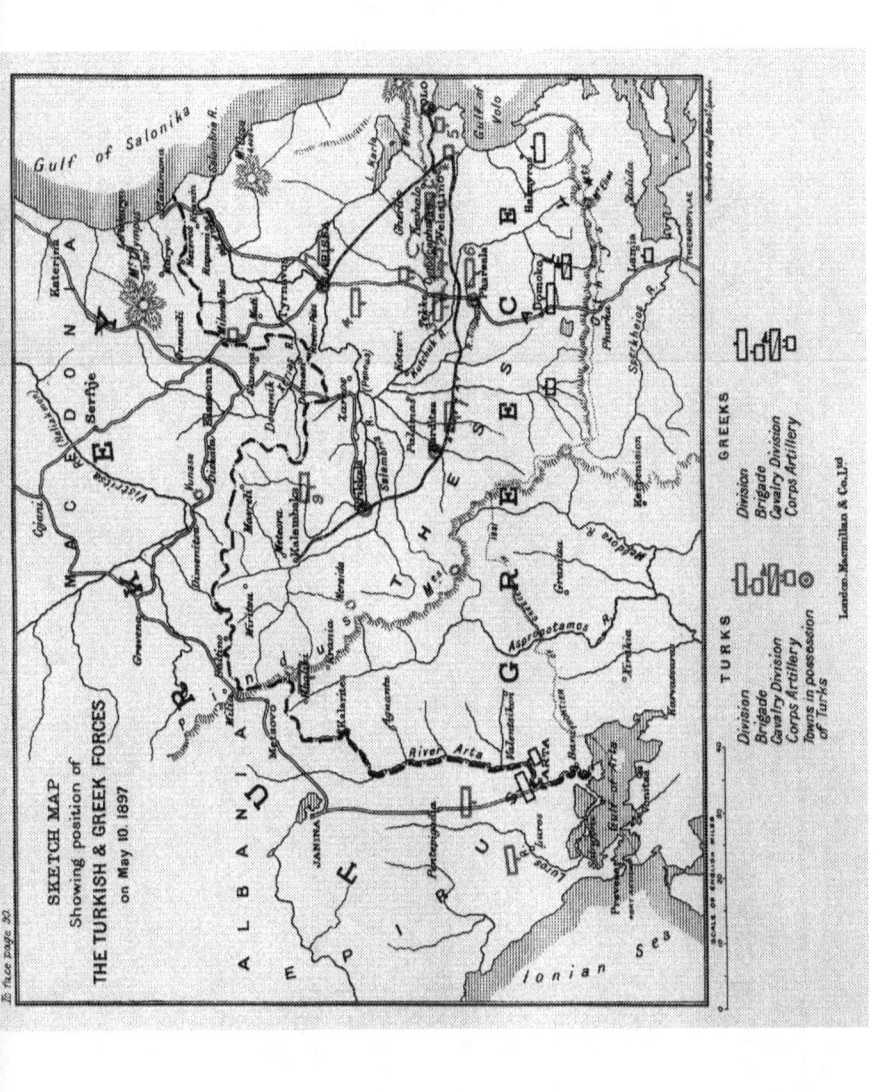

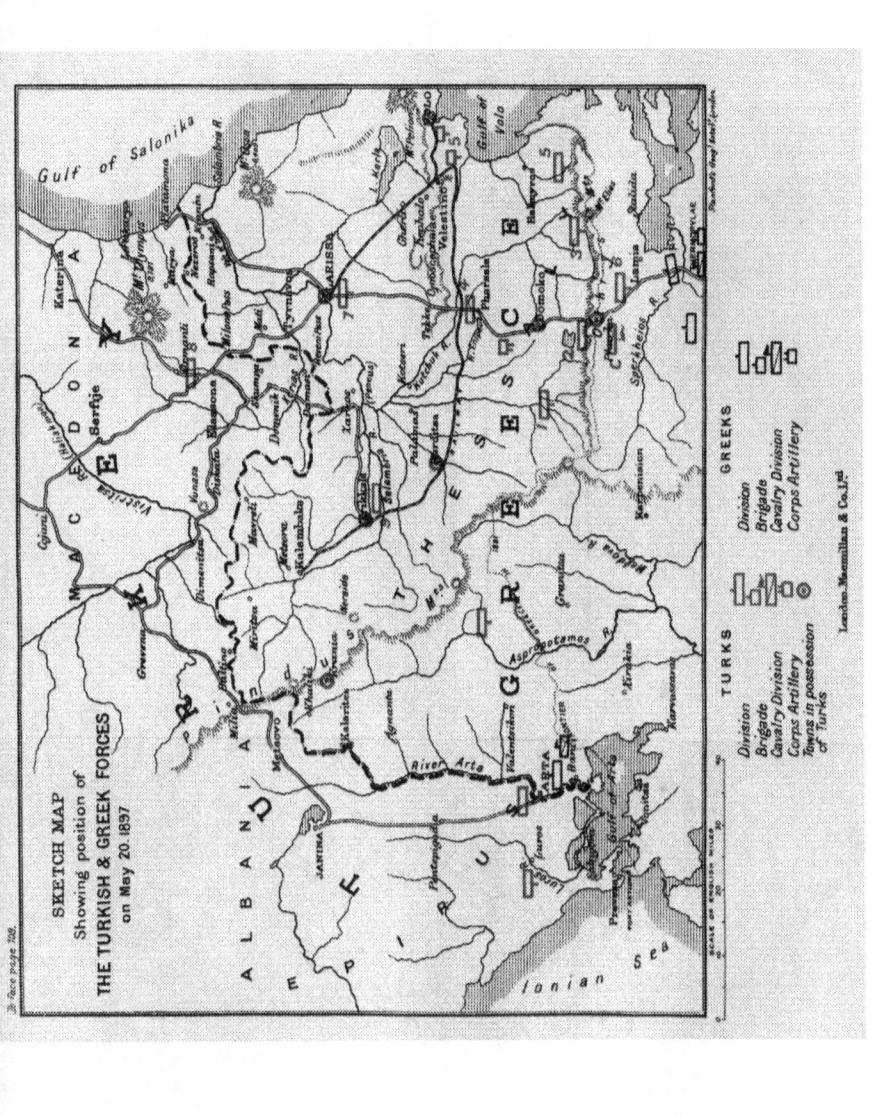

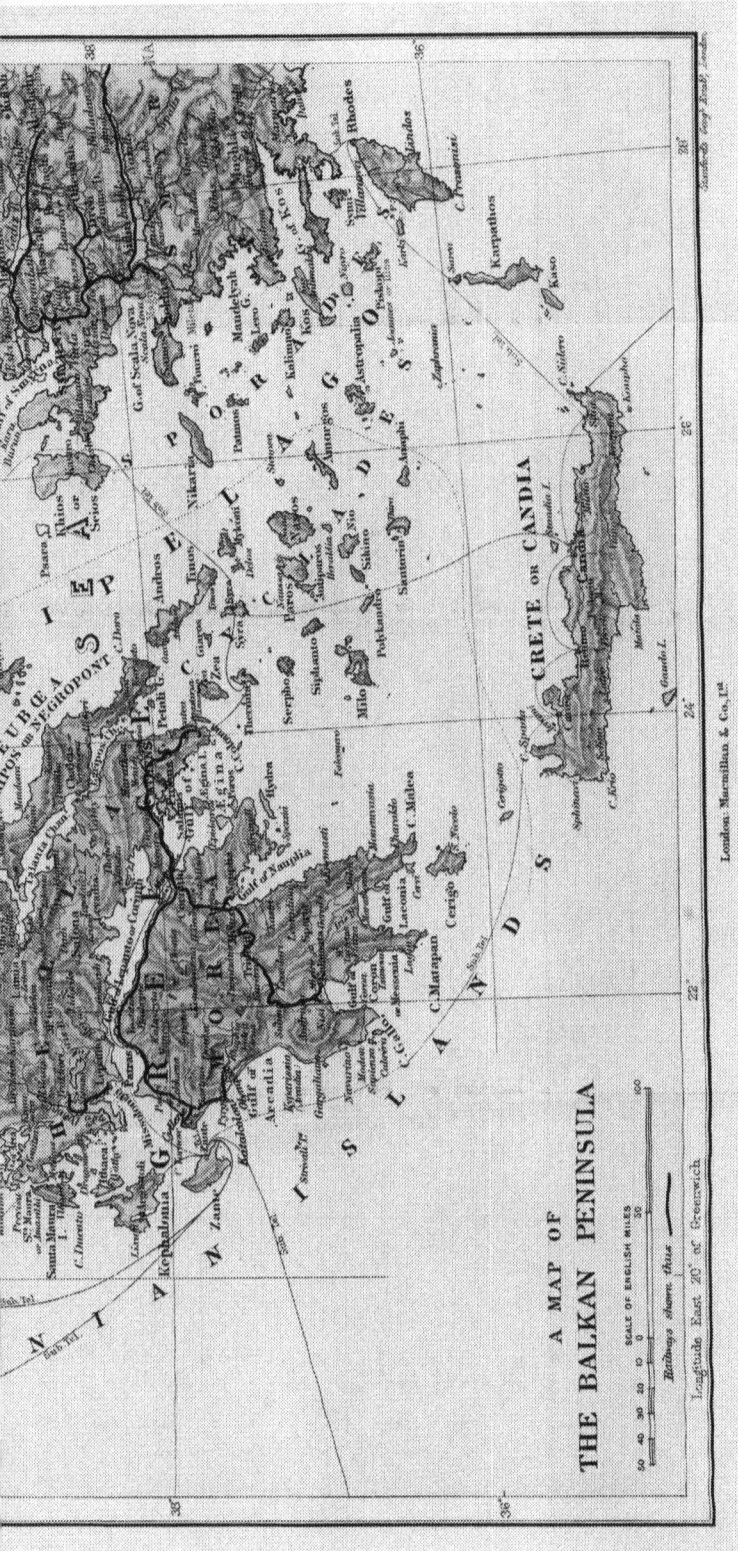

WITH THE TURKISH ARMY IN THESSALY

CHAPTER I

THE CAUSES OF THE WAR

EARLY in March it became patent to the general public of Europe that the Cretan question had ceased to have a merely local significance. The landing of Greek troops under Colonel Vassos had not only succeeded in fanning the flame of insurrection in that island into a serious revolution, but it had for the moment stultified the projects of reform laid down by the ambassadors, and had provided the admirals with an extremely difficult and hazardous task. But this was by no means all. It was evident that hostile preparations on a much wider scale were contemplated, if indeed they had not been made, in the Balkan Peninsula, and that the Hellenic Government were determined to use all the means in their power to provoke a conflict on the Macedonian and Albanian frontiers, and it was more than hinted that they would be materially aided by the disaffection said to exist in those provinces.

On the other hand, the Sultan's friends insisted that he had a fair and reasonable *casus belli*, and though quite willing to use diplomacy to its breaking strain, and thereby to emphasise their moderation, they relied confidently on a military force, their knowledge of which presumably justified their hopes.

Acting, therefore, on advice which professed to be more technical than political, the Porte commenced to mobilise the Army Corps in Macedonia, and ordered the division at Janina to be brought up to war strength, the alleged justification being that the presence of raw levies and bands of brigands in Thessaly necessitated precautionary measures of a defensive character. Once, however, that the ball had been set rolling, its rapid increase in size and speed proved that the Turkish Government intended to be ready for all eventualities, whether in their own or their neighbour's territories; and the concentration of troops in Northern Greece, pushed forward with apparently equal celerity, left no doubt as to the desires if not the intentions of the Cabinet at Athens. By the middle of March we were informed that there were no less than 50,000 soldiers round Elassona, the town which Edhem Pasha, the "commander-in-chief of the Turkish forces in Macedonia," had selected for his headquarters. Half this number were said to be at Janina, the capital of Albania.

The Greeks were reported to be massing at Larissa and Trikkala in Thessaly, and at Arta in Epirus, and were estimated as likely to reach nearly the same figure. Their fleet was arming, and encouragement in the shape of cheap sympathy and in the more solid form of material assistance was being furnished from all parts of Europe; Turkey also was taking her navy in hand, and was receiving more slowly and less spontaneously similar help.

In the meantime the warships of the six Great Powers were blockading Crete, though without any remarkable success, and European statecraft was devoting itself to preventing if possible the outbreak of hostilities. If it had only had to deal with constituted governments this endeavour might not have been abortive, but there was an element which was incapable of control, and which shortly eluded all restraints and brought on the war—I mean the Ethnike Etairia.

This was a Secret Society scattered all over Greece and the Levant, and comprising among its members officers and soldiers, politicians and diplomats, and working on the impressionable populace of Athens by all the sentiment, oratory, and mystification which generally appeal to a Southern race in a very marked degree. It had a reputation for wealth and influence, probably true, and for ability and organisation, certainly false, and its good will was thought so vital to the King's Government that it was allowed to have forces of its own in the field.

It had been established two years before with the avowed object of recovering to Greece the provinces of Macedonia and Epirus, and its agents had been disseminated over those parts of Turkey. After its apparent success in Crete, it was encouraged to try and force the hand of the Cabinet with regard to Turkey; but when it found itself likely to meet with opposition it cut the Gordian knot by raiding with its own troops across the frontier, with the inevitable result of a declaration of war.

It has now sunk into well-merited disrepute and obscurity, with the record of having been no less distinguished in the history of Greece for folly than for criminal meddling and incompetence.

The Hellenic population of Macedonia, and for that matter the Turkish population of Thessaly, are factors that need hardly be taken into account. Both were, to the best of my belief, quite contented and happy with their lot, and were far more occupied with the prospects of the harvests than with the autonomy of Crete. Any idea of insurrection that may have been fomented by Greek agents in Macedonia was at once knocked on the head by the visible and overwhelming presence of the Ottoman troops, and as we know never took any tangible form. In Epirus there was certainly some discontent and even mutiny among the Albanians, but to appreciate the value of this one has to understand the Albanian character, in which private plunder and personal vendettas hold far more central and important positions than any dynastic, religious, or racial considerations. The Turks to some extent know how to make use of these subjects of theirs, but are far too wise to rely on them, and are generally more exercised with excusing their conduct to Europe than with suppressing the anarchy that appears indigenous to the soil.

Macedonia then was quiet, Albania in its normal state, Constantinople nervous, while Thessaly and the major part of Greece, though really contented, were ready to follow the lead of Athens. That city, from the temperament of its populace, the ephemeral éclat of Crete, and the machinations of a number of demagogues and political societies, was noisy and bellicose. The European Powers were dilatory, due perhaps to the fact that they were not as united as they appeared to be, and one or two of them may have surmised a possible accession of influence or prestige from a war. Roughly speaking, this was the situation in March, a time when the snows begin to melt, when the climate in South-eastern Europe is most temperate, and when the mountain passes, the rivers, and the roads become practicable for the passage of large bodies of troops, and for their guns and baggage. In another two or three months a sultry summer would begin, water would get scarcer, and there would be the crops to look after, a very important item at any rate to the Greeks. If, therefore, there was to be a fight it must be at once, and this was no less realised by the parties concerned than by the onlookers; accordingly every nerve was strained by the generals to prepare rapidly for war, while diplomacy more irresolutely did its best to preserve peace.

Everybody was aware that active hostilities between Turkey and Greece might mean very serious complications throughout Europe, and possibly a much greater and more disastrous war, and indeed it was only because of the laudably correct attitude maintained by the Balkan States and the very strong line taken by the Great Powers that such a war was averted. Still there was a feeling that the air needed to be cleared and the contumacy of Greece to be chastised, while both the belligerents, despite their declarations to the contrary, evidently desired to try each other's strength, or at any rate to prove their own.

This is all that I would say about the political situation—a series of platitudes which seem necessary before dealing with the war itself. In the succeeding chapters I shall endeavour to describe the campaign in Macedonia and Thessaly as I saw it, only alluding to the course of events in Epirus when obliged to do so.

It is, of course, extremely difficult to avoid sympathising with the troops one accompanies, and most battles can be looked at from two points of view. I can therefore only promise to give an unprejudiced account of the war to the best of my ability, leaving the reader to judge of its actual fairness.

On March 18th, being in London on a short holiday from St. Petersburg, I was asked by the management of the *Times* to go out for them as Special Correspondent with the Turkish army. I obtained the necessary permission from my superiors at the War and Foreign Offices, and left next day, with such kit as I could collect in twenty-four hours, and on March 22nd I arrived at Salonika.

CHAPTER II

THE BASE OF OPERATIONS

SALONIKA, the ancient Thessalonika, lies at the head of the Thermaean Gulf, at the north-western corner of the trident of Chalcidice. It has a population of some 160,000, three quarters of whom are Jews, the remainder being Mussalmans and Greeks.

It is the chief town of the vilayet of the same name, and also the headquarters of the 3rd Army Corps, which, until latterly, radiated from Monastir. Built on the slope of a wooded hill, with a fine white stone quay and several beautiful old Roman archways, it hardly needs the glittering blue waters of the Aegean Sea, stretching away across the gulf to snow-capped Olympus and pointed Ossa, to give it that extraordinary fascination which the Byzantine cities of the Mediterranean always appear to possess. When I got there the weather was already warm, and promised to become hot very shortly, and indeed in less than a month the thermometer continually marked over 90°. Fearing the effects of the heat, the Turks were particularly occupying themselves with extending and increasing their hospital arrangements, as the last time that troops had been concentrated in southern Macedonia there had been an epidemic of typhus, and the plain of Elassona was notoriously insalubrious in summer. Accordingly one of the first places I visited was the large military hospital outside the town, where there were then four hundred beds. They were not, of course, all full, but preparations were being made on a large scale to supplement the existing accommodation, for the place was to serve as the general medical depôt of the army. It is an establishment that would compare favourably with anything of the kind in Europe, the wards, the doctors, and the system being all of the very best; for the Turk is inherently clean, and he is capable of having organisation drilled into him, both of which virtues are not to be despised. This hospital, however, was a sort of show place, and the temporary arrangements with divisional headquarters and in the field, which I saw later, did not come up to the same standard. Indeed they very often left much to be desired, and there is no doubt that but for the magnificent undertaking of Sir Edgar Vincent, who sent out the Red Crescent, under the auspices of the Ottoman Bank, many of the wounded, who, as it was, quickly recovered, would have died, or at any rate have suffered permanently from the effects of their injuries. But at the time that I saw the Salonika Military Hospital I was more occupied with endeavouring to discover what proportion of the troops passing through on their way to the front had fallen sick and been left behind, and I was astonished to find how small that proportion was, not ·5 per cent. The great mass had come hundreds of miles from the interior of Asia Minor, travelling either by road or in cattle trucks; they had then had a sea voyage of one or two days, and finally more road and more train with very little rest in between.

It showed at once that the general stamina was very sound, due, no doubt, to the remarkably healthy life the peasants lead in the provinces, and perhaps to their abstemiousness, for their physical wants are very small, bread and water—the latter frequently far from clean—being sufficient to support the majority. As, however, the men were fed extraordinarily well throughout the campaign, getting meat, rice, and soup every day, as well as tobacco, the clean bill of health that distinguished the army is easily explained. Malingering did not appear to exist, and men would often go on for a long time without reporting themselves sick—natural enough in a war. Most of the patients at Salonika were suffering from gastric diseases, with a certain proportion of ophthalmia, but syphilis was almost nil— I think only about one per cent. The doctors were evidently well up to their work, and appeared to have a good practical knowledge of medicine, though their surgery is not, as a rule, so successful. The assistants were kind and handy, and the stores plentiful. A larger medical staff, and a better organised system of hospital transport, and especially of field ambulances, are the chief real needs. The idea of the thing and the way to do it are already understood—*il n'y a que les hommes qui manquent*. Every one prefers to fight, and that is why all the technical services in Turkey are as yet in their infancy. There is, however, no reason why the German system should not be as well applied to these as it has been to the combatant arms, and no doubt after the experiences of this year this will be done. But on the whole there was very little fault to find.

The other main feature of interest in Salonika was the railway and the concentration of troops. The single line from Constantinople, by Dedeagatch to Salonika, had only been working some ten months, and the rolling stock was very limited. With the utmost strain the Austrian company could not manage to run more than five trains a day. Yet, during the whole of the month that the mobilisation went on, this extra service was kept up without any material delay in the passenger traffic, and with only one accident, which resulted in a block of thirty-six hours. The men were put in big empty vans or in cattle trucks, forty to a waggon. Each van could take eight horses or four field guns. A train averaged twenty waggons, and could therefore transport a battalion without its pack animals.

Accordingly it took about a week to send a division down the line, while the same distance by march route would have taken ten or twelve days. Altogether it was a most creditable performance, and, like the hospital arrangements, gave one a good first impression of the way operations were to be conducted.

Let us now glance at the Greek base. The Greek base was theoretically the sea, and practically the line of seaports extending along the coasts of the Aegean, for Volo, Halmyros, and Lamia, or rather Stalida, all served as military depôts, where troops and supplies were landed either in their advance or retreat. The lines of communication were thus always comparatively short, and not exposed to flank attacks in the same way as the Turkish provision routes from Salonika to Elassona and Larissa. The Piraeus served as a naval base, but in no case did Athens directly furnish the land army with supplies, the transport being carried on entirely by sea.

It will thus be seen that the whole essence of the Turkish plan of advance should have been a prominent and disproportionately strong left wing, with which to achieve the first principle of strategy by driving the enemy away from his base or cutting his lines of communication. This, however, was never realised, or at any rate successfully applied, and accordingly the Greeks were continually able to fall back on a seaport, take to their ships, and reform further south with a fresh and securer base. This however is somewhat premature, and will be discussed later.

I had excellent opportunities of seeing what was going on, thanks entirely to the unceasing kindness of Mr. Blunt, C.B., our Consul-General. Starting life as Lord Lucan's interpreter in the Crimean War, he has been wherever anything of interest has taken place in Turkey for the last forty years, and his untiring energy and unique knowledge of the country fit him peculiarly well for the important position he occupies at present. Mr. Blunt introduced me to the Field-Marshal commanding at Salonika, Kiazim Pasha, and also to the Vali, Riza Pasha, both of whom helped me in every way they could, and were as hospitable as they were kind.

At first there was some considerable difficulty in getting leave to go up to the front, but at last, by dint of telegraphing to London and Constantinople, an Iradé was obtained and I was informed that I could go to Elassona, but that my telegrams would be subject to the military censorship and that I must consider myself under military law. This was a natural and inevitable condition, and I accepted at once. I had got an excellent dragoman, Herman Charry by name, a Pole, who seemed able to talk every language under the sun, and I trusted to getting horses and grooms at Elassona. As for clothes I was rather badly off, having left everything in St. Petersburg, but before I came out I had ransacked my younger brother's wardrobe, whose absence at Oxford precluded any practical enforcement of his objections. A Norfolk jacket, two pairs of riding breeches, some boots and shirts, a saddle and a revolver comprised my kit—a fez, a necessity, I bought, and also such tinned things as I could get in Salonika. Finally, I took as much gold as I could carry in a waistbelt, in Turkish liras, and set out on March 31st in one of the Imperial torpedo-boats called the *Nusret*, to cross the gulf to Katerina. This boat had been most kindly lent to me by Kiazim Pasha, and as we steamed away in the early morning making about twelve knots, the captain pointed out the Kara Boyun headland where earthworks for siege guns had been erected, and whence started the line of submarine torpedoes that protected the entrance to the roadstead. We had a fairly rough passage and got to Katerina at nine o'clock. Here the Kaimakam very kindly supplied us with horses and an escort of Zaptiehs. A Circassian lieutenant of cavalry was travelling with me, and we at once set off on horseback across the northern shoulder of Mount Olympus to ride the forty miles to Elassona. The country was magnificent, great wooded valleys covered with pine trees and below broad stretches of greensward along the banks of rushing streams. The peasants were for the most part Vlaks, of the Roumanian stock, dressed in blue jackets and white skirts. They were nearly all occupied in building up the bridges and remaking

FRONTIER NORTH OF METEORA.

the roads, which were not in very good condition. Such of them as could talk Turkish seemed perfectly happy and contented, and told me that there was more trade and more transport going on than had been known for ten years, and that they were well and regularly paid for their beasts and their labour. We passed one or two Greek villages, where the inhabitants were more silent and a little frightened, but they seemed to be utterly lacking in any idea or desire of an Hellenic rising. There were comparatively few troops on the road, as it was not a main artery to the front, though at Katerina there were large grain, biscuit and sandal stores, and two or three thousand recruits being drilled.

We got to Elassona late that evening, and were hospitably lodged and entertained by the Governor. From what I had seen coming down to Salonika from the Servian frontier at Ristovatz, by Uskub and the Vardar, and from the state of the country between Katerina and Elassona, and finally from what I heard from other correspondents coming in along the ordinary route by Kalaveria or Sorovitch and Serfije, I came to the conclusion that any chance of an insurrection in Macedonia was exceedingly remote, and that even should it take place it would be promptly and effectually put down. The real interest lay in front and not behind, and within three weeks the Turks were over the frontier and nearly all the activity was transferred to Thessaly.

CHAPTER III

THE ARMY IN THE FIELD

The Turco-Greek frontier is about 200 miles long. Starting from the Aegean Sea, just south of latitude 40°, it runs west thirty miles to Elassona, dips twenty to the south, and going another twenty to the west returns to its original latitude near Diskata. From here it continues west again thirty miles more to Metzovo, where it turns south-west and at Kalarites due south, until it reaches the Ambracian Gulf at Arta.

This entire boundary laid down in 1881 follows the water parting of a high range of hills, the passes being for the most part in the hands of the Turks.

The line is almost equally divided by the great Pindus range of mountains that runs north and south and cuts it at Metzovo. The eastern portion of the Turkish territory is called Macedonia, the western Albania, the most southerly part of the latter, between the frontier and the Ionian Sea, being Epirus.

Thessaly consists of the three Greek provinces of

THE ARMY IN THE FIELD

Larissa, Trikkala, and Arta, the second being the largest and the last by far the smallest, and their southern frontier, slightly north of latitude 39°, marks the limit of the Ottoman dominions prior to 1881. The Turkish population has migrated to a very large extent, much more so than the Greeks have from Macedonia and Epirus.

It will be seen, probably much quicker from the map than from my description, that a sort of wedge with a broad head goes down into Greek territory between Larissa and Trikkala—its area being about 400 square miles and consisting of three plains, Elassona to the north, Domenik to the west, and Damasi to the south. In this wedge the great mass of the Turkish force was concentrated, as being able to meet an attack from either flank.

It will now be necessary to give a few details about the strength of the army, but they shall be made as short as possible. The figures are the actual and not the nominal ones.

```
        4 Companies make    1 Battalion or   750 men
        4 Battalions   ,,   1 Regiment  ,,  3,000  ,,
        2 Regiments    ,,   1 Brigade   ,,  6,000  ,,
2 Brigades (at 6,000)                    ⎫
1 Squadron (at 120)                      ⎬ make 1 Division or 12,500
3 Batteries (at 6 guns and 80 men)       ⎭
Non-combatants (say 140)
```

Roughly, however, one may reckon the fighting strength of a division at not much over 10,000 men —the remainder being employed for transport, supply, baggage, and as camp and quarter guards and depôt troops.

Besides the above infantry units a cavalry regiment consists of five squadrons or 1,000 sabres and an artillery battalion of three batteries. I shall, however, limit myself as much as possible to the words battalion, battery, squadron, brigade, and division.

At the beginning of April the troops in Macedonia were disposed as follows :—

1st Division, commanded by	Hairi Pasha	at Domenik
2nd " "	Nechat Pasha	" Skumpa
3rd " "	Memdoukh Pasha	" Elassona
4th " "	Haidar Pasha	" Elassona
5th " "	Hakki Pasha	" Diskata
6th " "	Hamdi Pasha	" Leptokarya

An Independent Brigade, commanded by Mahomet Pasha at Elassona

The Cavalry Division (15 squadrons), Suleyman Pasha, at Ormanli and the Corps Artillery (12 batteries), Riza Pasha, at Elassona.

The 7th Division, under Husni Pasha, arrived at Elassona on May 4th, and an additional brigade also arrived at Diskata about the same time.

The 8th Division, which never took part in the fighting, was not concentrated at Elassona before the 20th May.

Besides all these there were two strong divisions of 15,000 men apiece in Epirus, one at Janina and the other at Luros, under Ahmed Hifsi and Mustafa Pashas respectively, the former being in chief command. These had their own corps cavalry and artillery. There was, however, no real co-operation between the two armies until after the battle of Domoko, when the forces in Epirus had also been put under Edhem Pasha. During nearly all the campaign his command merely extended from the Aegean Sea to Metzovo, while everything west of that was directed from Janina.

The general strategetical idea, to use a very ponderous phrase, was as follows:—The base of operations was Salonika and the railway line running thence by Kalaveria and Sorovitch to Monastir. Elassona was the headquarters of the eastern and Janina of the western army. Katerina, Kalaveria, Sorovitch, and Serfije all served as depôts for recruits and *matériel* of the former force, though on a comparatively small scale, as everything was pushed forward at once.

Edhem's plan was to concentrate the great mass of his troops in the wedge, and merely to protect his wings with a sufficient force to guard against any flank attack. In any case he could easily move reinforcements to the right or left, while from the position he held between Larissa and Trikkala the Greek centre was seriously threatened. It was true that his lines of communication were not particularly well supplied with stationary troops to repel an attack from the sea, but there was a continual movement along them, and the Turks relied on the lack of numbers in the Hellenic army which would render any landing on a large scale impossible. South of Elassona lay two divisions, and round it two and a half more. The cavalry was at Ormanli, a village ten miles to the north, and the 5th and 6th Divisions were thirty miles or so to the east and west. The passes themselves were not held in any very great force, though the garrisons of the various blockhouses had been doubled; but all the available artillery positions had been armed with mountain or field guns, and though no regular system of outposts was adopted, single battalions were scattered along the reverse slopes of the mountains within a mile or two of the frontier.

The troops were under canvas, and, excepting two battalions in barracks, only divisional staffs lived in towns or villages. All transport and commissariat centred from Elassona, except those of the 5th and 6th Divisions, which drew direct from the railway.

The organisation struck me as distinctly good. Each battalion, squadron, and battery had its own pack animals which brought food forward day by day, fatigue parties being detailed from each unit for this service. There were small hospitals at Leptokarya and Diskata, and a large one at Elassona. Water was brought in in skins from the springs, and the men were not allowed to drink from the river that runs through the town.

Every man carried his own ammunition, never less than a hundred cartridges, and one rarely saw a soldier, whatever his employment, without his rifle on his back. Cooking, repairing, and armoury were all done in battalions, and in some ways the self-supporting elements were much better developed in the smaller units than in divisions. Divisional commanders rarely made proper use of their cavalry and artillery, and the employment of the technical arms they possessed, such as sappers, telegraphists, &c., was invariably directed from the army headquarters. In fact, the German system has not as yet grown much beyond the battalion.

The infantry, with the exception of the 7th and 8th Divisions and the 1st brigade of the 2nd Division who had the Mauser, were all armed with the Martini-Henry and long bayonet. Most of these rifles were made in America. The uniform was a fez, a blue tunic and trousers, generally finishing in putties, and sandals or soft shoes; these were much more useful than boots would have been, and did not appear to wear out. One hardly ever saw a case of footsore. Many, but not all of the men, had great coats, and all had cartridge shoulder belts and water-bottles. Such packs as they possessed they carried on their backs. The Albanian regiments always wore a small white skull cap instead of the fez, which they dislike. The uniforms were nearly all new, served out at Constantinople or Rodosto; the only men who had old clothes were among the regular active army, the Nizam, which constituted not a third of the entire force. Arms and accoutrements were kept sufficiently clean, but the kit was put on in the casual way that an Asiatic generally affects when dressed *à la franca*. The greater proportion of the infantry were Redifs or reservists, drawn from among the peasant population of Anatolia and European Turkey, the men averaging from thirty to thirty-five years old. Recruits and volunteers did not begin to come in until almost the end of the war. The battalions were nearly all drawn from particular towns and districts, a territorial system which struck me as excellent in every way. There were ten or twelve Albanian battalions, but the mass of the foot-soldiers were Turks.

The cavalry, on the other hand, included a very large proportion of Circassians and Bulgarian Pomaks—hardly any Kurds, and no Hamidieh regiments. They wore a black lambskin cap, a short blue jacket, trousers, and long boots, and besides a straight sword carried a slung rifle and cartridge belt. As a rule the men were much younger than in the infantry, averaging twenty to twenty-four, and were the most excellent material, good grooms and riders, and capable of becoming first-class troopers. The horses were mainly from Asia Minor, and averaged 14·3 to 15 hands; they were well looked after and fed, and even were, if anything, a bit too fat, as forage was nearly always to hand—generally chaff, oats, and grass. Saddles, and bridles *à la turca*.

Artillery, which was very numerous, was excellently horsed and gunned, but poorly trained.

TURKISH FIELD BATTERY IN LINE.

Six cannon, eighty men and sixty horses was the complement of a battery. The guns were $7\frac{1}{2}$ centimetres (3 inch) Krupp-Manteli, all in first-class condition, cased and clean, the limbers and gun carriages of the ordinary pattern. The shell weighed twelve and the shrapnel fourteen pounds, fired by time or percussion fuses. The horses were for the most part from Russia or Hungary, and ran bigger than those of the cavalry. The men, recruited from all parts of the Empire, did the manual part of their work well; but there was very little technical skill, and a battery had rarely more than one trained artillery officer. Three batteries of horse artillery armed with nine-pounders were attached to the cavalry division. These, however, were short of spare horses, so the gunners sat on the limbers and carriages; accordingly the speed was not very great. There were also three batteries of mountain guns on mules; first-class weapons, but the gunners very slow. Eighteen howitzers came up to Serfije, but were never brought any further, as there was no need for them. Taking it all round, the artillery, unlike the cavalry, was a very strong arm, but like the cavalry it was never made sufficient use of—the best work being done by the corps artillery which acted under the orders of Riza Pasha, who frequently used to borrow divisional batteries when he had need of them.

Among the technical arms the engineers were not prominent—such roads and bridges as were made being due either to the infantry or the civil population. The field telegraph was never a brilliant success, and the postal arrangements were lamentable. Of the two medical services the Red Crescent was excellent, but the army department on the march was frequently undermanned, and in action was rarely near the front. Supply, however, whether of ammunition, food, or forage, was quickly and efficiently conducted. The general staff knew and did its work creditably, but divisional headquarters were not nearly so well served. Such details as sketching and heliographing were barely practised, while balloons, machine guns, and military railways never existed at all.

Before closing this chapter, it may be well to give some details about the Greek army, gathered from the papers and from officers and correspondents who had seen it.

There were two brigades at Arta, Trikkala, and Larissa respectively, and smaller bodies at Kalambaka, Rapsani, and Volo—about 60,000 men in all —but reinforcements were continually being brought up, and towards the end of the campaign deserters were continually slipping away, so that accurate figures are hard to get at. At no time were the Greeks numerically as strong as the Turks.

The infantry were drawn for the most part from the reserve, and consisted of town and country people who knew little of soldiering and liked it less. The Euzonoi, light troops and mountaineers, were better stuff, fairly good shots, and with some training; they were, however, in a minority, and cannot have numbered over 10,000. The cavalry was very deficient in every way, and did very little throughout the campaign. The artillery was the best feature; though limited in guns, men, and horses, it was well drilled, and frequently made very good shooting, and among the officers there was more science than in the Ottoman Army. The technical arms were poor, the reserves of ammunition ludicrously small, and the arrangements for supply, transport and telegraphing distinctly bad. The medical service was to a great extent extraneous, and accordingly well managed. The Foreign Legion and the volunteers in Epirus were few in numbers, and appeared to be little better organised than the other troops, while the forces of the Ethnike Etairia were rather irregulars and bandits than anything else; they do not seem to have done much beyond causing the war and hampering the King's army when it had begun, being almost entirely lacking in discipline. All the men were armed with the Gras rifle, a somewhat obsolete weapon formerly used by the French army, ·433 bore, bolt action, and very liable to jam. The cavalry had carbines, and the guns, of the Krupp pattern, were good. The men wore a uniform resembling that of the French, with kepis, loose trousers and blue tunics, except the Euzonoi, who were dressed in their native kilts and fezzes.

Colonel Smolenski and Colonel Mavromichailis in Thessaly, and Colonel Manos in Epirus, appear to have been the most capable generals, but the staff was continually divided by the most extraordinary wranglings and mutual recriminations, and this no doubt contributed considerably to the demoralised state into which the army soon fell. At present, however, I do not contemplate giving further opinions on the Greek troops, and what I have stated above are little more than a few bare facts which appear necessary to the proper understanding of the campaign.

CHAPTER IV

EDHEM PASHA AND HIS STAFF

ELASSONA is a beautiful little town, lying at the entrance of a narrow green valley into a fertile plain watered by a winding river. On a beetling crag, just over the mosques and minarets below, is perched an ancient Orthodox monastery, said to be twelve hundred years old, and rich in the queerest old frescoes and eikons. Five solitary monks inhabit it, and from the windows of one of their cells I first looked out over the landscape where the Turkish troops were encamped, and beyond to the east, south, and west where high ranges of hills marked the frontier of Greece. To our left, but rather to the rear, rose the snow-covered tops of Olympus, and far to the right the peaks of Pindus seemed to join the clouds. Not five miles off to the east stood the col of Milona, the pass destined to see the first and fiercest fighting in the war; further down, towards the south, lay the defile of Skumpa, and beyond it again, but out of sight, the pass of Damasi marked the extreme southern point of Macedonia.

I had come up here with one of the Sultan's aide-de-camps, four of whom were attached to the person of the marshal, with power to report direct to Yildiz —a somewhat extraordinary arrangement according to our military ideas. This one, Nedjib Bey, was one of the cleverest and most intelligent men in the army, and if his fortune equals his abilities his career will be remarkable. In the afternoon he presented me to Edhem Pasha, who throughout the campaign treated me with the greatest kindness, and whom I shall always remember as the finest specimen of a Turkish gentleman I have ever met. He is now about fifty years old, a man of middle height, with a beard and moustache beginning to turn gray. His eyes and mouth are kind though firm, and he has a great sense of humour. Still, he is quite the grand seigneur, and his modesty is only excelled by his dignity. Starting life as an infantry officer, he so distinguished himself in the war of 1878 that he was promoted from the rank of colonel, which he then held, to the command of a brigade, and his defence of the Grevitza Redoubt at once gave him a name for courage. When the war was over he was appointed Vali of Uskup, in northern Macedonia, and during the years that he held that office his justice and clemency were no less celebrated than his bravery had previously been. He was afterwards Vali of Beyrout, and subsequently military commandant of the Zeitun district just after the massacres of 1894 and 1895. Latterly he has been

ELASSONA.

military governor of Crete, and in March of this year he was appointed to the command of the Ottoman forces in Macedonia. He is a field-marshal, and has now received the title of Ghazi, and the first class of the Order of the Imtiaz in brilliants, the highest decoration that the Sultan can bestow. Though most of his service has been with infantry, artillery is the arm of his predilection, and at first it was on his guns that he mostly counted for success. By nature he is extremely careful and methodical, having been brought up in the most conservative Turkish style,—he only knows a few words of French, —and accordingly his strategy was before everything sure, while his tactics were frequently slow. Of his ability there is no doubt, for during the whole of the campaign in Thessaly he not only invariably succeeded in defeating the enemy without suffering any material loss, but he managed at the same time to maintain his influence and authority in the army, and his prestige and popularity at the Palace, where many foes were continually at work against him, endeavouring to undermine both his power and his reputation.

It must always be remembered that hardly for an hour did the Commander-in-Chief have an absolutely free hand, and at one time nearly every movement of troops had to be explained to and authorised from the Palace before it was allowed to take place. In fact, Edhem had to avoid gaining a very great victory, and the consequent renown he would get throughout the Empire, as much as he had to avoid the least reverse to his arms or the least loss of men or *matériel*, which would have entailed instant disgrace. For him there were neither Malplaquets nor Sedans, his duty being to obtain the maximum of useful advantage with the minimum of personal fame.

But if Edhem was the Kurupatkin, Sefulat Pasha was the Skobelef of the war. Sefulat has been called by many the Moltke, but this to my mind is giving him too much credit. He has an immense amount of initiative and the glorious faculty of seizing the occasion, but most of the decisions were actually made by Edhem, and Sefulat had rather to snatch his *coups de main* out of his general's leisurely policy than Edhem had to supplement the achievements of his chief of the staff by the connecting links of careful strategy. Sefulat no doubt had better training and knew more of the theory and the theatre of war, but Edhem had practical experience, the responsibility of command, and the strength to make his will felt.

Sefulat Bey, for so he was called when the war began, was a colonel on the staff, a hard, dark, wiry man of three or four and forty. Born in Circassia, and brought up in Petersburg and Moscow, he speaks Russian, French, and German with equal facility. Five years ago he had been military attaché to the Ottoman Legation in Athens, and had subsequently acted as Consul at Larissa and

Volo. Here he had acquired a knowledge of the country and the language that were invaluable to Edhem Pasha, who after the battle of Pharsala raised him to the position of chief of the staff. He had already been made civil governor of Larissa, a general, and a pasha, after the taking of that town. He is a man of untiring energy, and possesses the quick and firm decision that is the first quality of a successful general. No doubt in the future, if he prospers at the Palace, his military career will justify its promise. Individually he is one of the kindest and pleasantest men I know.

To continue with the headquarter staff, Enver Bey, subsequently promoted to pasha and appointed governor of Volo, and Sabit Bey, another colonel on the staff, were both skilled and well-read men, speaking French and German, and endeavouring to supply the conduct of the campaign with the science of which it so sorely stood in need.

Riza Pasha, the commandant of the artillery, a man of not more than thirty-five, and educated for some time in Berlin, was, with his own arm, a capable and painstaking general. He was quick, he knew all his battery commanders, and he was a clever and experienced gunner. Suleyman Pasha, the cavalry general, did not appear to me to be in any way so well fitted for the post he held, though to what extent he was hampered by orders from making use of his division it is impossible to say. As it was, the cavalry only distinguished itself once, and then by a charge the folly of which was not excused by its bravery. This, however, was not as it happened Suleyman's fault. Of the divisional generals Hamdi Pasha was probably the most reliable and efficient. Neither Memdoukh, Haidar, nor Hakki impressed me much. Nechat and Hairi I did not know, but these two did fight battles on their own account, and won them, though at Domoko their tactics were almost culpable. Of Mahmud Bey I will speak later on, and also of Grumbkov Pasha, and this, with the exception of Nedjib and Mustafa Natik Beys, disposes of the most eminent persons in the army. The two latter were aide-de-camps of the Sultan; both of them were extremely clever, astute and well educated men, but their missions were more political than military.

Beyond those I have enumerated I do not believe there were twenty officers in the army who had a reasonable conversational knowledge of French, or more than the most elementary military training. This to a great extent was the reason of the minute supervision exercised by Edhem Pasha over his divisional generals whenever it was possible, and it explains the frequent tactical errors committed by commanders when acting independently.

The great mass of the regimental officers were either poor Turkish gentlemen, pleasant and brave enough, though not particularly skilful in their profession, or hard old rankers, men who had served thirty or forty years in the army, and had slowly risen to the rank of captain or major. These latter were very like sergeants in their ideas and methods, but they had a great hold over the men, and their courage and endurance were inconceivable. As a matter of fact the word courage is not strictly applicable to the Turk; he is, as far as I can make out, mentally impervious to any sensation of fear, and what passes with us for the most wonderful daring is rather a positive lack of any appreciation of danger. The Albanian, on the other hand, has a very shrewd idea of the damage caused by a bullet, and of the practical advantage of cover. This is, however, again somewhat premature.

CHAPTER V

THE INCURSIONS AT GREVENA AND KARYA

On April 5th the 1st Division moved its headquarters to Mologusta, six miles south of Domenik, and the 2nd Division received three battalions and a battery, which it needed to complete its strength. The day after an immense consignment of new boots arrived for the artillery, the fresh mountain batteries from Serfije were parked outside Elassona, and the 1st and 2nd Divisions each pushed forward half a brigade along the slopes of the southern and south-eastern frontiers.

At the Milona pass, which we used to ride up to nearly every afternoon, things seemed very quiet. The Turkish lieutenant in command of the post, Yunnuz Effendi, used to take us over to tea with the Greek officers in the opposite blockhouse, where he used to dwell upon the delights of war with realistic details, to the evident disgust of our hosts. He had passed twenty years in the army, and possibly the slowness of promotion had embittered his spirit, for though an excellent good

CH. V THE INCURSIONS AT GREVENA AND KARYA

fellow in many ways, he was bloodthirsty enough for a Kurd, and killed, I believe, over twenty of his quondam neighbours in the Milona battle. When on the frontier we sometimes used to go a little distance into Greece; one could see Larissa quite distinctly, though not Tyrnavos, which lay round a hill. Often we watched the troops exercising in the plain below, or, what was much more interesting, the Euzonoi and Albanians dancing opposition dances round their blockhouses, hand in hand, to the accompaniment of a reed pipe.

In the morning one visited the various divisions and some of the outposts, and in the evening I used to dine with Sefulat and Nedjib, or with the Kaimakam, who had most kindly given me a house.

On April 10th Mr. Hamilton Weldon came out as special correspondent for the *Morning Post*, and for the remainder of the time I lived with him; Colonel von Sonnenburg, an officer of the German general staff, joining us on May 6th.

At Elassona we were given a house, at Larissa we hired one, at Pharsala we appropriated one, and at Volo we found a hotel. Our food was generally mutton, with rice and bitter country wine; bread at times was scarce, especially at Pharsala, but latterly fruit was obtainable, though it is never particularly safe in the East. The sleeping accommodation was for the most part clean, but on one or two occasions it was more filthy than anything I have ever come across in the heart of Armenia or

Kurdistan. Unfortunately our tinned provisions very soon ran out, and as getting things from Salonika was a very long job, and buying in Larissa was almost an impossibility, we had to go without. But until we got to Pharsala there was hardly any illness, and then what there was, due to bad water, was, I fancy, limited to the Europeans. Luckily neither Weldon nor I suffered. To revert, however, to the events of the war. On April 9th we were startled by the news of what has generally been called the Raid of Grevena.

Grevena lies about sixty miles to the west of Elassona and some distance north of the frontier, and the raiders in point of fact never got there. The details were as follows. On the night of the 8th a party of about 1500 men, composed of Corfiotes and Alexandrians with a good many Greek deserters, left Kalambaka under the auspices of the Ethnike Etairia, and crossed the frontier at Baltino. The lieutenant commanding the Turkish blockhouse, who had a force of only thirty men under him, ordered them to halt, and appealed to the Greek frontier officer, who said it was no business of his as they were not King's troops. The greater portion of the band had by then passed the actual line, and some of them soon came into contact with a picquet of the 5th Nishangi and a fight began. Who fired the first shot no one will probably ever know, but a combat went on all night in the woods on the mountain

v   THE INCURSIONS AT GREVENA AND KARYA

sides, and the Turks were gradually driven back. The Greeks burnt the two blockhouses behind them and drove out the garrisons.

They had advanced three or four miles by dawn when they were met by three companies of the 6th Nishangi from the 5th Division at Diskata, and at the same time some of the Turkish troops from the line of unfired blockhouses attacked them in rear.

They then appear to have lost their discipline, for the greater part of them were very soon surrounded and fifty or sixty were killed. The remainder cut their way back, but reformed at the frontier where they halted. The Turks did not pursue them in consequence of their orders and from lack of troops. Eight Turkish prisoners were taken to Kalambaka, and one Greek, or rather Corfiote, was brought to Elassona.

On the 10th nothing more was done, but on the 11th the band again set fire to two blockhouses, and a skirmish took place along the crest line of the hills. Islam Pasha, who commanded the brigade, and Sefulat Bey, who had ridden from Elassona, had by this time got a sufficient force to the front, and moving forward they drove the brigands back some two miles, and the raid was for the time ended. After this we at Elassona thought that very possibly the whole thing would be explained by the Greek Government.

On the 13th, however, and again on the 14th a fresh

incursion of Greek regular troops was made near the Shuma Monastery Pass east of Damasi. In the middle of the night the Turkish sentinel on the heights challenged some men he saw in the gorge below, and was answered in Greek. He called his officer who happened to know a little of that language, and the voice explained that a company of Euzonoi had lost their way. After some further parleying the men retired, and the affair when reported at Elassona was not looked upon as very grave. But exactly the same manœuvre was repeated next night, and the Greek officer then said that the territory he was on was not Turkish. On the Turks threatening to fire he again retired with his men, but next morning when the Ottoman troops began to erect stone intrenchments along the head of the gorge, the Greek lieutenant, who commanded a stronger body in a better position, threatened on his side to fire unless the work was stopped, as it was, he said, contrary to the agreements laid down in the Treaty of Berlin.

We heard all this on the 15th, and it then appeared obvious that not only the Ethnike Etairia but also the Hellenic Government were bent upon forcing on war, so that when on the morning of the 17th came the news of a fresh incursion the night before at Karya we were not particularly surprised.

Weldon and I at once got leave to go to Karya, taking with us an officer and a trooper whom Edhem Pasha had very kindly told off to accompany us. It was about twenty-four miles off, and we did it in two

GREEK ADVANCE ON KARYA.

hours and a half, as the sound of cannon told us it was something more than a raid. The road lay along the lower slopes of the chain of mountains that culminates in Olympus, and below that peak we found the little village of Karya occupied by Hamdi Pasha and the best part of his division. His batteries unfortunately were at Leptokarya, and he had only four guns, which he brought into action soon after midday.

The story was much the same as that of Grevena, except that the Greeks were all regulars. They had passed the frontier in the evening, before the Turks could bring up a sufficient force to hold them in check. A desultory wood fire had continued all night, and in the morning it became evident to Hamdi Pasha, who had come from Leptokarya, that the number of troops opposed to him was large enough to justify his bringing up the major part of his division. The roads, however, were extremely bad, and he had eventually to get artillery from Elassona.

In the meantime—it was now about two o'clock in the afternoon—the Greeks had got well inside the Turkish frontier, and a regular battle had begun. The scene was a long, green valley running east and west, about half a mile broad from slope to slope. On the north rose the bare, brown shoulders of Olympus capped by snow, and at its foot lay the little village of Karya, surrounded by tents and alive with men.

On the opposite hillside, which was covered with pine and beech woods, a scattered fight was going on right up to the crest line, where the blockhouses marked the frontier.

The infantry fire was fairly, but not very, heavy, and the short battery, not well supplied with ammunition and poorly posted on a little plateau, was not working with any great speed or doing much damage.

I got Hamdi's leave to possess myself of the military wire and laboriously proceeded to telegraph in Turkish to Sefulat at Elassona, and to beg him to retranslate my message into French and start it off to London. This done, we delivered ourselves to a more detailed contemplation of the fight. We first of all visited the temporary hospital, a necessary, but most painful duty, and were as astonished by the fortitude of the men (they never had anæsthetics even under amputation) as we were pleased by the care and skill of the surgeons. We then climbed up to the battery and the infantry supports, the men of which were lying down and eating and smoking according to the custom of the Turkish soldier. Here we took a few photographs, and watched the shooting. By this time it was getting well on into the afternoon, and as there was no likelihood of the fight finishing that evening and every probability of something happening in the neighbourhood of Elassona, we decided to go back there before it got dark.

Accordingly we said good-bye to the general and wished him luck, and started back on our ride. He had then nearly nine battalions engaged and three in reserve, and on the road we met four more and two sadly needed batteries. As we neared headquarters, we found all the troops in camp along the hills behind Elassona parading for a night march, and when we got in at eight o'clock and went up to the Field-Marshal, who was just going to have dinner, he hailed us with the news that war had been declared at five o'clock that afternoon, and that "to-morrow, Inshallah, we shall be on the road to Yenisheyr (Larissa)."

CHAPTER VI

THE BATTLE OF MILONA

THAT same evening of the 17th April the cannon on the heights below Menektépé and Kritiri came into action, and their dull roar went on all night. Extremely little execution was done, however, the gunners being apparently content to pull the lanyard and trust to Allah for the result. About midnight the Greek infantry, who had been able to mount the winding military road on their side of the Milona Pass without much loss, crossed the crest line and began to descend towards the plain of Elassona. At the time I was occupied in printing French telegrams (printed characters and French being a *sine qua non* for the telegraph clerk), so that I can only speak of what I heard. But it is apparently certain that the Greeks descended two or three times almost to the level ground before they were finally driven up again by the Turkish infantry.

In the small hours of Sunday the 18th the Greek Consul in Elassona packed up such effects as he could put on a horse, and, accompanied by a Turkish escort, set off on his adventurous journey to Larissa, where he arrived safely, I believe, later in the day. Directly dawn broke, Weldon and I rode off towards the Milona Pass, and about a mile from the foot of it found five batteries of the corps artillery in action under Riza Pasha. They were endeavouring to shell the enemy's troops just over the crest line at a range of 3,000 yards, though I think it was really considerably less. Shrapnel was not used at all, and at first the firing did not appear to be very well judged, though in the afternoon the results were much better. Edhem Pasha had not then come out, but Sefulat was there, and also Memdoukh, whose division was in front.

We left the guns behind and rode on up the path with a Circassian trooper until we got into the entrance of the pass. Here the first bullets began to pass over our heads; but from the sing we judged them to be spent, and as we had not yet come on any visible signs of conflict we went on. About three hundred yards higher up, as we were getting into the more rocky part, we came upon a poor chap with his face cut to pieces by a bit of shell and quite blinded by blood. He was being helped along by a friend, who informed us that there was "chok shey" (a lot of work) up on top, and advised us to avoid the Albanian battalions, who "did not know giaours." We now began to come to an occasional corpse, and the bullets got a good deal more frequent. We pushed on, and round the next turn of the pass found two companies in support waiting to mount the slope. They had their ammunition mules with them, and were occupied in the most methodical way eating lumps of bread and smoking, though the fusillade from Menektépé was stronger than ever. I asked the captain why he kept his men in such an exposed place, but he said, "Binbashi bizi borda brakdi" (the colonel left us here), which was for him an excellent and all-sufficing reason. Weldon took a photograph or two and we went on, but thought it now better to dismount and leave our horses in a little gulley with our trooper and another orderly we had met. We were now not more than a hundred yards from the head of the pass, and about twenty yards beyond us stood the tree which marked the last turn. We got there, and then began to crawl on our hands and knees, until at last we found ourselves level with the firing line, who were lying down in extended order just below the hill top. The blockhouse was about fifteen yards in front and was in possession of the Turks, while the Greek blockhouse fifty yards further on was empty. Behind it, however, was a long low stone wall, from which came the enemy's fire; and every now and again a shell from Riza Pasha in the plain plumped down beyond them, but we could not see with what result. The noise was tremendous all the time from the rattle of the musketry, the roar of the cannon, and the whistling of the bullets.

We were not particularly *bienvenus* with the firing line, who were Albanians, and after asking us who we were, and why the devil we had come, they advised us to retire, which we accordingly did, after Weldon had rendered them immortal with his camera. We found our horses and went back to the captain, who was persuaded to let us climb up the hill with his company, which was at last going into action. We rather stupidly took our horses along with us, and mine, having attained a commanding and extremely prominent position on the hill top, refused to be led down, and I was for ten minutes much divided between my duty to him and my newspaper. At last, however, I persuaded him to descend, and we then picketed them and went up again, whereupon two Albanians took up their position behind us with their fingers on the triggers of their rifles. Not desiring to serve as cover we again retired, and as the firing had slackened considerably, mounted and rode back to the corps artillery, where we found Edhem Pasha and the headquarter staff sitting on the ground in the sun and watching what could be seen of the fight. Here we were informed that a battle had begun at Damasi, where Hairi had some difficulty in keeping the Greeks back, and that Nechat Pasha at Skumpa was attacking the Greek batteries posted on the heights to the west and north of Tyrnavos. About midday a fresh message came in from the Second Division to the effect that Hafiz Pasha, a fine old soldier who had served in the Crimea, had been killed while leading his brigade into action on horseback. No further news arrived from Damasi that day, or at least we heard none, but a continual fusillade went on along the hill tops, while the artillery on the Turkish heights and that in the plain kept up its fire. This continued all the afternoon without any decisive result, until at last about 4 P.M. the first battery of the corps artillery blew up one of the Greek blockhouses with a shell. It was a beautiful shot, and Riza Pasha himself laid the successful gun.

The Turks then drove the enemy a little down the hill, and Haidar Pasha, who had hitherto only had half his division in action, now sent up his remaining brigade. At seven the fire slackened sensibly, and by eight there was nothing but a desultory fusillade with occasional cannon shots, so we rode back to Elassona to eat and sleep a little. The battle was not, however, over until midnight, and slight firing continued from Karya far away on the left, where Hamdi was still fighting, to Damasi at the southern point of the frontier, where Hairi was opposed to the mass of the Greek artillery from Zarkos. During the night two more battalions and two batteries were sent to Karya, and the Independent Brigade was brought to the foot of the Milona Pass, so that nearly all the troops were pushed forward to the front line. At four o'clock in the morning, as we

GREEKS BELOW MILONA.

were saddling our horses to ride out again to the scene of action, an orderly rode in and presented us with the following note, which I reproduce in full, as of some interest :—

"Mon cher ami,
"Son Excellence le Maréchal m'ordonne de vous informer que toutes les hauteurs à partir de Menektépé juscequ' à Skumpa, excepté Kritiri, viennent de tomber au pouvoir des troupes impériales.
"Tout à vous,
"NÉDJIB,
"*Aide de Camp de S.M.I.*"

This was the official announcement of the conclusion of the battle; and cantering out we found Menektépé deserted and the Milona col occupied by the Sultan's troops, who were engaged in burying the dead and repairing the fortifications by the blockhouses. The sight was a sad one, and a great change from the excitement of the day before.

The infantry had rested and eaten during the night, having been fighting for thirty hours, and the Greeks were now found to have evacuated Ligaria or Karadéré, the village at the eastern base of the pass. The heights of Kritiri, however, still remained in their hands, and the news from Karya showed that Hamdi had not so far done anything more than drive the enemy back to the frontier, although he had been fighting continuously since the night of the 16th.

In front of Skumpa the Greek batteries had been

dislodged from four of their positions, but no considerable advance had been made, and at Damasi what result had been obtained was not more favourable to the Turks. That day (19th) the corps artillery moved right up to the foot of the pass, and passed the Independent Brigade, which remained in camp behind it. The Cavalry Division was advanced from Ormanli to the plain of Elassona, and the field telegraph was continued along the Milona road, and brought up to the head of the pass. Two extra batteries were sent to Nechat Pasha, who was ordered to co-operate in the bombardment of Mount Kritiri which dominated Tyrnavos, and the remainder of the corps artillery, with the mountain guns, were directed on the reduction of that position. Nothing very much, however, was done on the Monday, as everyone was tired out, and the expenditure of ammunition had been so great that fresh supplies had to be brought up. Nearly all the troops had been in the firing line, and had completely used up their battalion reserves, while the divisional ammunition had been left at Elassona. It was not, as it happened, a matter of very great importance, as the Greeks were evidently far worse off; indeed, in some respects it prevented any further waste, as fire discipline and any check on the cartridges used hardly existed. There was no lack of morale, but on the other hand there was very little attention to putting up sights or aiming, and collective was entirely subordinated to independent firing. In the attack up the hills the extended formation was adopted rather by instinct than command, for when a company advancing in line found itself inconveniently hustled by the enemy's bullets it merely spread out a bit more. But the absolute imperturbability of the men, their unhesitating and unwavering advance in the teeth of the most murderous fire, and the casual way in which individuals halted for the most ordinary purposes under a hail of shrapnel, convinced us that the result of the war was a foregone conclusion. It is hard for a European to imagine even the most highly trained troops displaying such *insouciance*; and the only explanation to fall back on is the original hypothesis that fear is an influence to which the Turkish brain is not susceptible.

The battle of Milona was then completely terminated by the small hours of the 19th, the crest line remaining in the hands of the Turks; this and the battles of Velestino and Domoko were the only actions of a sustained character and on a large scale during the entire campaign, as in the other fights much smaller bodies of troops were engaged. Edhem Pasha very wisely waited to recruit the strength of his men, and did not hurry them on at first; but this was probably the only occasion on which his careful strategy was altogether beyond blame. Menektépé had already been deserted, but Kritiri still held out, and its reduction and the subsequent events up to the taking of Larissa I purpose to deal with in the next chapter.

CHAPTER VII

THE ADVANCE ON LARISSA

The weather now began to get hot, and no rain fell, while for the next four days we enjoyed an experience almost unique in these days of large operations and long range weapons. We sat on the grass at the summit of a commanding height and watched, spread out below us on the plain of Larissa, the progress of Edhem Pasha's tactics. It was a *kriegspiel* on a grand scale, enlivened by the knowledge that it was all real, and that the map and the pieces were factors in the destinies of Europe. No movement had taken place on the side of Trikkala, so it soon became evident that both generals were concentrating their attention and their troops on Larissa; and the evolution of Edhem's careful advance was not rendered less interesting by its slow rate. The first thing to be done was to reduce Kritiri, where the Euzonoi had strengthened by every artificial means within their power a naturally strong position. Along the heights of a scarped cliff their intrenchments bristled; below

THE ADVANCE ON LARISSA

lay a rocky gorge, and beyond it, on our side, rose a long reverse slope, which served the enemy as an admirable glacis.

Again and again did the Turkish guns bombard the heights, and again and again did the Albanians rush down the slope and endeavour to scale the cliff; but the fire poured on them from above was murderous, and the batteries behind them had little effect on parapets of rock and stone.

When at last, on the night of the 23rd, the enemy's troops abandoned a position which had only been rendered untenable by the loss of its food supply, we found how few Greeks had been killed, and how formidable were the lines behind which they had been intrenched.

Kritiri, however, did not command the road from the Milona Pass to Karadéré nor the road beyond. It was a strong position, which precluded any direct attack on Tyrnavos, and which checked any advance through the defile of Skumpa, but beyond that it was not of any great offensive value, and probably many generals would have masked it in front and rear, and left it behind.

After several abortive assaults Nechat Pasha decided to bring such a fire to bear upon it as would at any rate exhaust the enemy's ammunition supply for some time, if they replied, and with this object a cannonade and fusillade were concentrated on it during the afternoon of the 20th and morning of the 21st, which surpassed in volume and vehemence anything I have ever heard—even the *finale* of a public schools field day at Aldershot. In consequence, during the whole of the 22nd, the Greeks remained quiet, and the advance of the Turks in the plain on the 23rd no doubt made it clear to them that any further delay would end in their envelopment. Accordingly that night they retired from their heights, and passing through Tyrnavos, fell back on Larissa, relinquishing a position which, if carried by assault, would have cost the Turks several thousand men.

The history of Kritiri then need be no further considered, as it had no material effect on the Turkish advance beyond the delay it involved. We will return to the main body.

On the morning of the 20th, after the troops had had one day's rest, the Cavalry Division, with its horse artillery, crossed the pass and descended into the valley beyond Karadéré. They advanced about a mile and a half and then the artillery unlimbered and began to fire at a small mamelon, behind which the Greeks were supposed to be in some force. This portion of the plain resembles a V in shape, of which the arms are about three miles long, the fork being the place where the pass debouches. Beyond the V the valley broadens out into the flat basin of the river Peneus, Larissa being directly in front and Tyrnavos round the right-hand bluff. The country is cornfield and grass, intersected by two tributaries of the Peneus, the left bank of which is

THE BATTLE OF MATI.

[*To face p.* 53.

bordered by five or six woods, where the Greek infantry had taken up a fresh position in support of their artillery, which lay near the mamelon. Beyond a few shots very little was done on that day, but in the evening and during the night the Third Division and the Independent Brigade descended into the plain, and a fresh brigade from Diskata, under Hakki Pasha, arrived at the Turkish foot of the pass.

On the 21st, the morning was occupied with the bombardment of Kritiri, but about midday the Greek guns in the plain opened fire on our horse batteries, and this has been called the battle of Mati. At the same time we could hear heavy firing on the far left, which augured the advance of Hamdi.

A methodical cannonade continued in the plain until four o'clock in the afternoon, when everything ceased, as if an understanding had been come to that both sides should have their evenings free. On the Turkish side (in the plain) there had been no casualties at all, and on the Greek one man had been killed. This is, of course, nothing to do with the bombardment of Kritiri, which was well away to the right.

No further movement was made on that day, and early in the morning of the 22nd, the Third Division deployed and advanced on Déliler, a small village, which it found empty, and then occupied, as it had done to Karadéré. Under its cover the Independent Brigade moved away to the left in column, in order to effect a junction with Hamdi Pasha. At the same time Hakki Pasha's brigade from Diskata, which had now been augmented by three fresh battalions from Salonika, and will be henceforward styled the Fifth Division, advanced in support of Memdoukh.

The cavalry, acting as a screen and accompanied by its guns, had succeeded in forcing the Greeks to retire from the mamelon to the woods, but without any serious engagement. That evening we had news from Hairi that his troops were now alligned along the southern frontier, and that the enemy was falling back on Larissa.

In the meantime the Fourth Division had been working hard at a military road which they were constructing up to the head of the Milona Pass, and the corps artillery now began to come over, the guns being dragged up the last ascent by fatigue parties of fifty men each.

On the 23rd Hairi was ordered to advance and to wheel to the left with one brigade, and Nechat received the same orders, though his brigade advanced direct. Mahomet (commanding the Independent Brigade) effected a junction with the extreme right of Hamdi's division, and the cavalry in front pushed foward another two miles to the environs of Tyrnavos.

These movements were, however, effected very slowly, and as it was extremely misty all day from the heat it was impossible to follow them in detail. Weldon and I, however, rode down into the plain as far as within two miles of the mamelon, but were not allowed to get close enough to see any fighting.

All day a strict censorship was applied, and no telegrams were allowed to leave Elassona.

That night the Greeks deserted Kritiri, and the heads of the columns of the First, Second, Third and Sixth Divisions came on to the arc of a circle drawn from Larissa. That night also, as we subsequently heard, took place the panic flight of the Greeks from Tyrnavos to Larissa, so well described by Reuter's correspondent with their army.

We were soon to see the signs of it.

In the morning of the 24th the cavalry, advancing with much circumspection, found Tyrnavos absolutely empty, and accordingly occupied it with four squadrons, the remainder of the division bivouacking outside. It was still feared that a grand resistance might be made along the banks of the Peneus; and Edhem Pasha, though he rode into the town, did not sleep there, but returned to Karadéré, where the telegraph line had now arrived. The Greeks, by the way, had omitted to cut their line from Karadéré to Tyrnavos, and a clerk was accordingly sent on to the latter town to take charge of the office.

In the evening Grumbkov Pasha, a German officer employed in the service of the Sultan as Inspector-General of Artillery, who had come out to follow the operations, obtained leave to send forward a single squadron to reconnoitre. The squadron, commanded by Jaffer Bey, advanced to the suburbs of Larissa and took prisoners four Greeks, who gave themselves up. These men, belonging to the Crown Prince's regiment of the Guard, told Grumbkov that Larissa was practically empty of troops, that the civil population was panic-stricken, and that he would have no difficulty whatever in occupying it.

Under these circumstances, and without waiting for orders from the Field-Marshal, he borrowed six squadrons and a battery from the cavalry general, and advanced soon after dawn against the city.

Near the banks of the Peneus, which was almost dry, some firing was heard, discovered subsequently to have come from the convicts who had been released from the municipal prison and furnished with rifles; accordingly one gun was unlimbered and three blank shots were fired over the town which immediately became perfectly quiet.

Grumbkov and Sefulat, who was, as he always was, well to the front, thereupon entered by the west gate, and were immediately welcomed by the Mussulman population, numbering some four hundred souls, and by the Jews, who had trusted to their religion for their safety. The citadel, the government house, and the bank were at once occupied, but the railway station was found denuded of all its rolling stock, and no use could therefore be made of the line; Edhem was notified of the course of events, but pending his orders no measures were taken for the pursuit of the enemy, and vedettes were merely thrown out a mile to the east and south of the town, Mustafa Natik Bey becoming military commandant. This was on the Sunday morning (25th).

On the news arriving at headquarters, the following orders were issued :—

1st Division to advance on Zarkos.
2nd   ,,   to support it on the left.
3rd   ,,   to encamp at Larissa.
4th   ,,   to halt at the Milona Pass.
5th and 6th Divisions to skirt Larissa to the left, and
    bivouac five miles beyond to the south and east.
Cavalry Division to be one mile in advance of last
    two divisions.

These movements to be completed by the night of the 26th.

Weldon and I rode into Larissa on the Sunday, and found it in a condition that quite bore out the accounts of the Greek flight. The shops were broken into, the private houses were looted and in the greatest disorder, the barracks were half burnt, and even the big guns in the citadel, with their ammunition, had been left to the victors. More; the wounded soldiers and the sick in the hospitals had been deserted by the military doctors; and as the Turkish medical officers did not arrive until next day several of the patients died in the interim, unknown of and untended. Altogether it was a deplorable example of panic and *débâcle*, and did much to convince the sober troops that saw its results of the unworthiness of the foes against whom they were pitted.

During the night an Albanian battalion that had been rather foolishly allowed to enter the town gave some trouble, and the whole of the general staff that had arrived spent their time patrolling the streets and forcibly preventing plundering. In the morning two men were condemned to be shot; and from then until the time I left there was no pillage worthy of the name, the isolated acts that did take place being committed by a few irresponsible marauders, who limited themselves to sheep stealing and once or twice setting fire to cottages.

This completes the sequence of events from the Battle of Milona to the taking of Larissa. The only advances which have not been followed in detail are those on the extreme right and left. Of these Hairi Pasha, who had at first been driven back a little, but had readvanced on the 20th, had maintained a slight and desultory fight during the 21st and 22nd; the Greeks then began to move off to their right, and not to the rear, for when he took Zarkos he found it deserted. Hamdi Pasha, with the Sixth Division on the left wing, had had a much more arduous task,—indeed his troops were practically fighting all the week, and at first it appeared that the Greek attack from Rapsani and the Vale of Tempe might seriously endanger the success of Edhem's advance. As soon, however, as it became clear that this advance was progressing, the Greeks understood that any delay in the retreat of their right wing would result in its being cut off, and accordingly it fell back on Larissa during the 22nd and 23rd. The fiercest fighting at Karya and Nezeros had been on the first two days of the war; latterly, as Hamdi brought up the entire strength of his division, and pushed forward the fresh batteries that he had received from Elassona, his preponderance in men and guns changed what was originally a stubbornly-contested battle into a slow but steady retirement.

Up to the 25th the Turkish losses were estimated at about 400, and the Greek casualties at not much more, these including the deaths in the flight from Tyrnavos. In the Ottoman army the expenditure of ammunition had been enormous, and the superhuman efforts that were made to bring up cartridges at the expense even of food, showed that this was thoroughly appreciated. It was estimated that in the first week nearly three million cartridges were fired. These figures, however, were never officially furnished, and it is impossible to gauge their accuracy at all justly.

CHAPTER VIII

THE OCCUPATION OF NORTHERN THESSALY

WE now enter upon the first of those inexplicable waits, which, however much they may have commended to Europe the Turks' humanity, did not increase their reputation for strategy.

For four days nothing was done beyond the occupation of Zarkos, which town Hairi found deserted. Then came the first Battle of Velestino, neither intended nor directed by Edhem, resulting in a reverse. This was followed by another pause of four clear days, after which the rapid successive falls of Pharsala and Volo inaugurated the final and longest interval of inactivity, lasting over a week. This was at last terminated by the Battle of Domoko.

It is impossible to say to what extent diplomacy and orders from Constantinople influenced this policy, but regarded from a purely military point of view it was almost inexcusable, and even the lack of cavalry could not justify the absolutely passive *rôle* which the stronger and victorious army saw fit to play. Pursuit was ignored, and the "strategic advance of the

GREEN MOSQUE AND BRIDGE OF LARISSA.

CH. VIII THE OCCUPATION OF NORTHERN THESSALY 61

columns," to use the official phrase, meant little more than the necessary pushing forward of the first line to make room for the reinforcements that were daily pouring in.

Larissa, or Yeni Sheyr (New City), as the Turks call it, is a pretty town lying in the centre of the historic plain that is bounded by Olympus, Ossa and Pelion. To its north the river Peneus rushes through the Vale of Tempe to the sea, and on its south the crags of Cynoscephalæ conceal the plain of Pharsala and the river Enipeus.

The traces of its classic part have, however, almost entirely disappeared, and the frequent and dominating minaret well typifies the hold that Islamism still maintains in Thessaly. The green mosque by the western gate excels in architectural beauty anything else in the town, which depends for its picturesque element on the Mohammedan population. The Greek peasant in the fields does indeed wear the dress of his race, a costume as becoming as it is workmanlike. But the modern Hellene citizen is as disappointing in his appearance as in his ideas, and does not compare well with the honest and dignified Turkish merchant. We found many Greek deserters both in Larissa and Volo who were quite prepared to discuss the errors and incapacity of their generals, but equally unwilling to fight in their army or to subscribe to its funds. My impressions were hurried, and may have been prejudiced; but I did not care for the Greeks I met, and I believe that most Englishmen would have formed the same opinion.

Weldon and I, in company with Sir Ellis Bartlett and Colonel von Sonnenberg, were put in charge of the bank, where we had a guard, which we unsuccessfully endeavoured to initiate into the technique of sentry-go. But for all its lack of smartness it was extremely alive to the practical part of its duty; and the guttural "Yazak" (Forbidden) never failed to check the unwary intruder, even though the sentinel was apparently asleep.

The town in a day or two began to resume its normal appearance, though the shops remained shut for some time, and for the first week there was hardly any business done. The military commandant was soon superseded by Sefulat, now a Pasha, who united in his person all the functions of a general and a governor. An official rate of exchange was declared, security of property and person was guaranteed, and pillage was severely put down. Very little indeed took place; and the single house that was set on fire was saved by the efforts of a cavalry picquet, who were quickly on the spot.

The order of the day, however, was "Kef," the passive but quite temperate form of repose into which the Turk seems naturally to sink after any unusual spurt of activity. Every sort of report favourable to the success of the Imperial arms was afloat, and nearly all were countenanced by the authorities; one adventurous squadron from Suley-

VIII THE OCCUPATION OF NORTHERN THESSALY 63

man Pasha's division did actually ride beyond Velestino, and this was immediately magnified into the capture of Volo, and passed as such by the censorship. The weather became extremely hot, and the energy of the headquarters staff seemed to be affected by it. In fact, as the Eton Latin Grammar used to pithily express it, *Hannibal cum victoria posset uti, frui maluit.*

Hairi Pasha on the right leisurely advanced on Trikkala, whence the Greeks had fled, and he took it on the 30th. Nechat and Memdoukh gradually shifted their camps until they found themselves half way to Pharsala; and Hakki accompanied by Suleyman Pasha, who was said to be "sweeping the country with his cavalry," had got to Gherli, six miles north of Velestino, by the 29th. Hamdi lay in front of Larissa, and the non-combatant services filtered in day by day.

The most surprising thing was the extraordinarily friendly attitude adopted by the country people of the villages round about. A good deal was no doubt due to fear; but the peaceable attitude of the Turkish soldiery did much to creating a good impression among the civil population, and soon the Greek merchants and traders came stealthily back to the city. Even the most ordinary rights of war were not resorted to, and the sheep and oxen bought by the Turks, at any rate at that stage of the campaign, were paid for in hard cash. As Colonel von Sonnenberg used to reiterate to us, deploring the absence of a German army corps to show them the way to do it, *Sie wissen nicht Krieg zu führen;* and assuredly, though no one knows better how to fight, the Turks do not yet appear to have assimilated the higher ethics of the art of war.

In the meantime Katerina had been bombarded by the Greek fleet, and a certain amount of food supply, mainly cases of biscuits, had been destroyed. There had been an intermittent guerilla warfare up at Diskata, and the troops there had advanced to the support of Hairi at Trikkala. Grumbkov Pasha had returned to Constantinople, and Colonel Baron von Giesl and Captain Dupont the Austrian and French military attachés, were now at headquarters. Altogether it was a little dull; but late on the night of the 28th a young officer arrived whose advent was the signal for the single romantic episode in the campaign. This was Mahmud Bey, son of Kazi Mukhtar Pasha, the Ottoman High Commissioner in Egypt, and a Caterji Oglu, one of the oldest families in the Empire. Mahmud, who has been educated in Berlin, and has served in the Guard there, though only thirty years old, is a colonel and an aide-de-camp to the Sultan, and in a way he is already one of the most notable men in Turkey. Speaking French and German like a native, and thoroughly imbued with Western ideas, he is yet a most ardent patriot, and his desire to re-organise the administration of his country is no less marked by singleheartedness than by confidence in his ultimate success. To the obstinacy and pride of his race he has joined the energy and organising talent of the Germans; and if he can manage to steer his earlier career through the devious mazes of an Oriental Court, his fame in the future should equal his deserts. To him belongs the unfortunate glory of the first battle of Velestino, where a mistaken daring and the halting support of his superiors made him responsible for the single Turkish reverse of the campaign. Yet his general ability is beyond doubt, and his social qualities only heighten its value. His name has been freely connected with the Young Turkish party; and no higher recommendation could be possessed by that section of the would-be resuscitators of the Ottoman Empire than that they can lay claim to such a leader.

CHAPTER IX

THE FIRST BATTLE OF VELESTINO

THE evening he arrived Mahmud told Sonnenberg that he had been given leave to execute a reconnaissance in the direction of Velestino, where the Greeks were known to be in some force. He offered to take Sonnenberg; but as the latter could not go I was given the chance instead, and accordingly about four o'clock next morning, 29th, we set out with an orderly sergeant, a couple of troopers, and my Albanian cavass, a man whom I had picked up at Elassona, and who used to ride in to the telegraph stations with my messages. The weather was lovely, though as the day wore on it became very hot, and the country, covered with corn and grass and backed by the noble range of mountains that rises between Larissa and the sea, looked beautiful. Our ride of some forty miles was uneventful, except that we once lost our way while trying to take a short cut, and rode into a Greek village which lay to the north of Lake Karla and which had not yet been occupied by any Turkish troops. We were, however, very well received, the people all coming out and asseverating that the Ottoman rule was all that they desired, though how true this statement was it was hard to say. We got something to eat, and crossing the marsh that fringes the western point of the lake sighted Gherli about eleven o'clock. This was a little village on the railway, lying about half way between the lake and the Cynoscephlae range. Here we found a mixed force, consisting of eight battalions, four batteries, and six squadrons, under the command of Hakki and Suleyman Pashas. Both the infantry and cavalry divisions had been materially weakened by *troupes d'étapes* and transport detachments, which they had left on their road, and the cavalry, never strong, had been largely drawn on for escorts and postal services. Mahmud had got some sort of unofficial leave to " borrow " a sufficient force to execute his reconnaissance, but was not, I fancy, particularly welcome to the two generals, who were quite contented with their independent position, and not in the least anxious to bear any unnecessary responsibility. After a little delay Mahmud got two battalions, two squadrons, and a horse battery, with a promise of further support if he needed it; and with these we set out about two o'clock towards Velestino. Gherli, as I said, is a station on the railway from Larissa to Volo, which runs in a south-easterly direction as far as Velestino. Here it is joined by the line from Trikkala and Pharsala, and changes its course to due east. From Gherli to Velestino is nearly six miles, and from Velestino to Volo is about the same distance.

The position at Velestino was of considerable importance. Firstly, it was based on Volo, whence supplies and troops could be readily brought up by rail. Secondly, it commanded the junction, and behind it lay all the rolling stock of the line, which the Greeks had taken away from Larissa, while through it lay the only good road over the mountains to the sea. Thirdly, as long as it remained untaken any direct advance to the south made by the Turks would be exposed to the serious danger of an attack in flank.

The position was extraordinarily strong, as indeed were most of the positions selected by the Greeks throughout the campaign. A semicircle of hills, backed by the mountains of Pelion and Cynoscephalæ, stretched from right to left. In the centre of the arc a depression marked the col over which ran the road to Volo, twisting to the left or north in its ascent. At the foot of this col, but rather to its south, rose the white minarets of Velestino, the rest of the town being hidden from view by thick woods which extended from the slopes on our right away to the borders of the lake on the left. Beyond the lake rose the precipitous cliffs of Pilaf Tépé, on which the Greeks subsequently mounted six fortress guns.

It was known that Velestino was held, but by what force was uncertain. A troop of Turkish horse reconnoitring in its environs the day before had been driven back by infantry fire; but we could not judge whether the Greeks intended making a stand, and at that time, just after the taking of Larissa, a very poor estimate was held of their morale. We advanced in column along the southern slopes until within two miles of Velestino, one squadron of the cavalry acting as a screen on the front and flanks, and the horse battery following immediately in rear of the second squadron. The chord of the arc of hills was here about five miles long. The troopers beat up the cornfields and the lower slopes of the hills to our right, but found nothing. They did not however go as far as the woods; and on getting to a point where the main road from Gherli joins the track along which we had come, they halted, while the battery mounted a small hill in rear and unlimbered.

It was then past four, and we could now see infantry moving along the crest line of the hill just over the town, but they did not appear to be numerous. One of our battalions deployed and advanced, the cavalry moving down into the level ground to the left, where they again halted. The Greek troops on the hill then began to fire; our infantry advanced and replied, supported by the battery, the latter's range being about 2,000 yards. After a few shots shrapnel was employed; and the Greeks, who had begun to descend the hill, halted under cover of the rocks and contented themselves with returning the infantry fusillade. In the meantime the cavalry had pushed forward towards the wood, and, on getting within 500 yards, were received with a smart infantry fire which emptied one or two saddles and sent them back to their former position. A Greek battery then appeared on a height more to our left, but still quite close to the town, and began to answer our artillery fire. It was now nearly six, and more infantry could be observed crossing the crest line. Altogether we reckoned the enemy must have three or four battalions ready. Mahmud accordingly sent to Hakki for reinforcements, and about seven a battery belonging to our cavalry division appeared in the plain to our left and began a desultory fire. It soon commenced to get dark, however; and as it was obvious that nothing could be done that night, "cease firing" was sounded, and we prepared to bivouac.

My Albanian had got hold of a filthy little cottage, where Mahmud and I entertained von Giesl and Suleyman Pasha to a dinner of two thin chickens, some bread and some bitter wine. Up to nine o'clock we were enlivened by a dropping fire from the enemy; and if one went outside to see after the horses, a spent bullet generally seemed to salute one. Very little damage had been done, however, and Mahmud had evolved a plan of turning the Greek left flank with his two battalions, which looked very hopeful.

We slept for three hours in the greatest discomfort from every species of crawling thing, and an hour before dawn the troops got under arms, and the infantry set out on its flanking march along the summit of the hills to our right. It was a difficult and slow business, and we did not expect them to get near to the Greek left for two or three hours. As the sun rose, however, firing began on the right, and shortly afterwards two Greek batteries came into action in front. The Greeks had adopted the same idea and had intended to turn our flank, and we were now in the awkward position of having our right wing unsupported and possibly outnumbered, and of being for the moment without a centre, as the troops which were to have come from Gherli had not yet arrived. One battalion, however, came up within the next half hour, and being sent forward in column along a very exposed slope, suffered severely from the enemy's shrapnel. The point of attack of this advance was a diminutive hamlet called Kephalo; but as the Greek infantry fire was very heavy, the battalion was ordered to halt in a fold of ground, to wait for Mahmud's advance on the right. Another battery now joined the Greek artillery, and some of their infantry advanced into a dip where we could see nothing of them. They were, however, mounting the opposite slope and constructing entrenchments at the top, where they occupied a position between our right wing and the cavalry in the plain.

By nine o'clock in the morning Hakki Pasha had

brought four of his battalions and two batteries into action down to the left and near the lake. Opposed to them was the enemy's force in the woods and some guns on the heights above. The combat between them continued all day, but no advance was made on either side, and the lake precluded any flank movement. The firing was seldom very heavy, and for the most part at ranges of five or six hundred yards. The Turks, however, being in ploughed fields, suffered more considerably than the Greeks, who were intrenched among the trees. Our right wing had still been unable to advance in any force.

At midday four squadrons which had been collected by Mahmud charged against the line of infantry fortified on the centre hill. It was a most foolish and useless act, and cannot be excused by the alleged supporting advance of the right wing. That wing had never made good its position, being outnumbered, and was at the time at least 1,200 yards away. There is, indeed, no doubt that if at that moment the enemy's intrenchments had been carried a general advance would have been possible, as the cavalry could have threatened the flank of the Greek batteries in rear. But cavalry was not the proper arm to employ in front, and the consequence was disastrous.

The 400 odd troopers rode across a level stretch of ground and up the slope of the hill at a trot, subjected the whole time to a heavy fire from the

The Battle of Velestino.

[*To face p. 72.*

shelter trenches. Had the aiming of the Greeks been even respectable, half the force should have been killed. As it was they lost some forty men, and within fifty yards of the infantry the trumpets blew the "retire," and the squadrons wheeled about and galloped back, which under the circumstances was the only sensible thing they could do. That the charge should have been made at all is inexplicable, and the only reason there can have been for it was that Mahmud perceived that unless the advanced Greek infantry was driven in before it had made its position impregnable, the Turks would have to retire. He used the only troops he had to hand.

After this there was a lull, and our right wing retired a little along the line of hills. At two o'clock a company of the enemy advanced to reoccupy Kephalo, which had been for some time deserted, but they were met and repulsed by the Turks. There was a little bayonet fighting, and a dozen or fifteen men were killed on either side, the Turks remaining in possession of the huts. This pause continued until nearly four o'clock, though the fact that since early morning four trains had been seen to come in to Velestino augured that the Greeks were bringing up reinforcements. This was soon borne out by a fresh infantry fire, which began again with all the violence of that of the morning, while at the same time the four Greek batteries poured shell and shrapnel on the Turkish guns, which were saving their ammunition. The fusillade from the heights also recommenced, and our right wing began to descend the hills, being quite outflanked by the enemy's force there. There was not, however, the least semblance of panic. The men, perfectly conscious that at least double their number of troops were opposed to them, strolled over the ground in the casual and nonchalant manner which characterises them under the most murderous fire. In the meantime the Greek artillery continued firing heavily, and two more batteries were brought up on Pilaf Tépé; so that it became obvious that as no fresh reinforcements had arrived or were as yet expected from Larissa, some sort of a retiring movement would have to be executed.

The Turks, however, remained in their positions until after six, when the infantry began to trail slowly back to Gherli, the artillery continuing the fire for another two hours. They then retired also, watched and followed by the powerful search lights of the warships in Volo harbour, which gave a weird effect to the scene. The Greeks did not advance during the night, and next morning the actual position was very much the same as it had been two days before, when we arrived at Gherli.

The conduct of the Turkish infantry in the battle was admirable, though I fancy their fire obtained little result, having regard to the expenditure of ammunition. The batteries were more useful, and more care was shown in laying the guns than I had hitherto noticed. The cavalry did all the work that fell to their share with courage, but squadron leaders showed no remarkable skill.

On the Greek side the infantry fire was destructive, and their artillery practice in the afternoon was well judged, and would have been much more effective if all the shells had burst, which they did not. More offensive tactics might possibly have resulted in some slight success; but the Greeks probably recognised that the forcing of the Velestino position by the Turks was merely a matter of days, and were satisfied with having fulfilled their duty, and gained, which they certainly did, a respite of a week. It was their most successful action, and made it clear that they could be made into good troops with proper discipline and officering. The stronger test of a defeat showed their lack of these requisites.

The expenditure of ammunition was as usual enormous, and out of all proportion to the number of casualties; it would have been even greater had the Turks not been compelled to husband their cartridges as the day wore on; for this became necessary because of the absence of any system of supply from Larissa. Some of the battalions were nearly run out of ammunition by the evening.

The reverse, however, was only discreditable to the Turkish generalship, for the position, against which a totally inadequate force was launched, was strong enough to merit the name, which it subsequently received, of a "second Plevna."

CHAPTER X

THE ACTION OF PHARSALA

THE first battle of Velestino was a brilliant fight, but except for its reconnoitring results practically useless. It may be regarded as an isolated event, which was not part of Edhem Pasha's general plan and which affected his advance very little. He had now fully appreciated the defensive position occupied by the Greeks and called their "second line," which I will once more briefly describe, as its idea must be understood to explain the subsequent strategy. This line was to all intents and purposes the railway from Pharsala to Velestino. The main base was at Volo, in rear of the latter position, but another line of retreat lay open, should it be needed, to Domoko. Here the Greeks could be joined by such troops as had retired on Volo and the sea, and here also they could again close the land approaches to Athens. As long as Pharsala held out, Volo acted as the supply depot, but directly the army retired the base was transferred to Lamia.

The railway from Velestino to Pharsala, after

THE ACTION OF PHARSALA

winding in and out of a narrow range of hills for a few miles, runs along a broad and level valley. On the north rise the heights of Cynoscephalæ, beyond which lies the plain of Larissa; on the south are the outlying peaks of the Othrys. Between these and the railway and parallel to the latter flows the Enipeus river. The Greeks were concentrated in force at the two ends of the line—their force at Velestino being estimated at 12,000 men and that at Pharsala at double that number. In the centre several batteries and a small body of infantry were posted on the heights of Cynoscephalæ. The extreme right on Pilaf Tépé was very strong: guns of position had been dragged up the heights, and on the lower slopes Smolenski had intrenched his infantry on all sides.

The rest of the position at Velestino was also, as I have said, very formidable, and the Greeks evidently expected there the main Turkish attack. The same, however, could not be said of Pharsala, for though the plain supplied an excellent glacis, the town lay at the foot of a spur, and its western flank could be turned from the direction of Trikkala. The natural advance of the Turks would have been by Velestino, for had that town been taken first, the force at Pharsala would have been for the moment cut off from the sea and might have been enveloped, whereas by striking first with his right wing Edhem must infallibly drive the enemy back on their base.

The latter was, however, the plan he elected to

pursue, and it was carried out as follows :—On May 1st, the troops at Gherli were strengthened by four battalions, two batteries and a squadron, bringing the total up to about 11,000 men. This division for the present remained inactive, and practically merely served as a masking force. A continual accession of strength, however, went on during the next week, all the independent Albanian battalions that came in being sent on to Hakki, so that by the 7th he must have had 15,000 men under his command. On the 2nd, 3rd, and 4th the divisions that lay to the south of Larissa, those of Hamdi, Memdoukh, and Nechat, advanced on a parallel front until within five miles of Pharsala, meeting with no opposition.

On the 3rd Hairi's vanguard occupied Karditsa without any engagement, and on the 4th news arrived from Elassona that the head of the 7th (Husni's) Division had passed that town and that Islam Pasha was advancing from Diskata with 10,000 men in support of Hairi.

On that day a feint was made from Gherli, and two extra trains were in consequence sent from Pharsala to Velestino, presumably containing reinforcements; there was, however, little fighting.

On the morning of the 5th Edhem Pasha, who had gone forward with the headquarters staff to a village called Karademirtsi, directed a reconnaissance in force to be made across the Pharsala plain. This was supported by a general advance of the army.

The Turkish vanguard, consisting of four battalions, four squadrons, and two batteries, accordingly advanced and came into action with the Greek outposts in the centre of the plain about midday. The latter had the same amount of artillery, no cavalry, and half the number of infantry. A smart fight ensued, lasting for an hour and a half, when the enemy began to fall back on the railway line. The retirement was conducted slowly and methodically, and the Turkish cavalry failed to make any impression on its rate. The Greek artillery fire was exceedingly good, and the position along the railway embankment was held for another hour. By five o'clock, however, they were again in retreat and crossed the river as evening came on. The Turks did not advance beyond the railway, but waited for Hairi, who was a little behind the other columns, to come up into line. A dropping cannonade went on until dark, when there was silence, and the Greek bivouac fires could be seen blazing on the other side of the river. The Turks slept in the positions they had taken and advanced at dawn, but met with no opposition, and it soon became clear that the town had been evacuated. The Greeks retiring during the night along the road to Domoko had also left the heights immediately behind Pharsala unoccupied. Accordingly one brigade of Hamdi Pasha's division crossed the river and entered the town, and outposts were pushed forward a mile to the south. No pursuit, however, was undertaken. Nearly all the inhabitants had fled, leaving their houses empty, but four guns, a quantity of ammunition, and over fifty prisoners were captured. It was, therefore, assumed that the Greek flight had again partaken of the nature of a panic. That night two or three isolated cases of burning took place in the villages on the plain where no bodies of troops were stationed. These were due to small detachments of Albanians, who had been left behind by their battalions. Whenever an officer was present the discipline was admirable, and all the marauding that occurred was done by groups of four or five men. Most of the villages indeed were deserted by their inhabitants, who had carried off what they could, and beyond shooting the pigs, which was very needlessly done for amusement, and taking an occasional sheep, the Turks did little damage. There was, however, more laxity noticeable than after Larissa, and the fault lay in the inefficient organisation of the lines of communication where there was no thorough or efficient control. At the front everything was excellently managed; but on the road in rear a few irresponsible camp followers were inclined to give trouble.

The immediate effect of the action of Pharsala was that the Greek batteries that had been posted on the Cynoscephalæ hills retired towards Velestino, where Hakki had made a second and much more vigorous attack. He had indeed made a forward movement on the evening of the 4th, and had then retired, and this was construed into a Greek victory. He fought his battle next day, 5th, and the details I shall give in the next chapter. Husni Pasha, with the Afion Karahissar division, had now arrived at Larissa, and in the meantime another event of interest and importance had also taken place. This was the arrival of the Red Crescent contingent, which was alluded to in Chapter II.

The day after war was declared, Sir Edgar Vincent had telegraphed to me asking me to find out what medical assistance in the way of doctors or appliances would be most grateful and useful to the Turkish army. I saw Achmet Pasha, the Surgeon-General, and transmitted his requests to Sir Edgar Vincent, who mobilised in Constantinople, and despatched to the front in less than four days the Red Crescent. This consisted of a superintendent, six doctors, six hospital assistants, 200 beds, coverlets and mattresses, and an immense stock of medical appliances, drugs, dressings, etc. Journeying by way of Salonika and Sorovitch they chartered caravans at that place and came the remaining 160 miles by road, arriving at Larissa on April 30th. The whole undertaking was a triumph of organisation and speed, and its humanity and practical use did much to maintain British prestige and the idea of British wealth with a nation that appears likely to soon forget both.

The actual good done by Dr. Lardy and his subordinates was incalculable, as the Turkish hospitals were getting overcrowded and running short of material; indeed, I think it is not going beyond a reasonable figure to say that the Red Crescent saved the lives of at least two hundred Turkish soldiers. Some difficulty was at first experienced in assuaging the jealousy of the Ottoman medical authorities, but directly the Red Crescent was established at Larissa (and later at Pharsala and Domoko) it proved its own voucher, for every wounded Turk that came in asked to be sent to "Banka Khasta Khanési." The tales of the fortitude and endurance displayed within its walls are legion—one may suffice as an example. A Turkish soldier lying on the operating table was having his lower jaw cut away (as usual without an anæsthetic); in the middle, and at the most painful moment of the job, he stopped the surgeon, and pointing to a comrade who was lying hard by smoking and waiting his turn, "Never mind me," he said, "look after him; he wants a light."

CHAPTER XI

THE SECOND BATTLE OF VELESTINO

EDHEM PASHA had now got his right wing considerably more forward to the south than his left, and no further advance could safely take place until Volo was in his hands. The possession of this place could never be of any real value to the Turks, as it was unfortified, and therefore at the mercy of the Greek fleet, should the latter decide to bombard it; but this eventuality was improbable, as the admiral had not enough men to effect any permanent landing, and a wanton destruction of Greek or international property must in any case accompany whatever damage the ships could do to the few Turkish troops that would occupy the town. Edhem had decided to send a strong force along the Pharsala valley to turn the Greek left flank, and at the same time to direct the main attack against Pilaf Tépé, and the hills behind Velestino. Hakki Pasha, now in command of a strong division, had moved forward from Gherli on the 4th, and there had been a little fighting, after which the Greeks had retired from their most advanced line of intrenchments, and Hakki had fallen back a mile. On the morning of the 5th he received news from Edhem that the 3rd Division should advance to his support, and that Hamdi Pasha would co-operate with him on his right flank. The Greek artillery on the heights of Cynoscephalæ would then be compelled to withdraw, and the moral effect of the loss of Pharsala would probably cause a further retirement on the part of the enemy.

Accordingly on the morning of the 5th May a very strong force of infantry, over 8,000 strong, supported by the fire of five batteries, commenced the attack on Velestino.

The Greeks had altogether four successive lines of fortifications rising one above the other up the slopes of the hills, and on the top of Pilaf Tépé they had mounted six guns in position, from which, by the way, no shot was ever fired. Otherwise the position was very similar to that described in Chapter IX, and it is therefore unnecessary to dwell at much length on the minor details.

A heavy and continuous infantry fire was kept up from the plain during the whole day, and the Turkish artillery occupying the more advanced mamelons was able after finding the exact range to search out the Greek intrenchments. The enemy had only mountain artillery, and some of this was concealed at first and necessitated the employment of indirect fire; here less effective results were

VELESTINO. [To face p. 85.

obtained. A forward movement was maintained by the Turks against Cynoscephalæ all morning, and by two o'clock in the afternoon the Greeks had retired from their second line of shelter trenches there without leaving any considerable number of dead.

Edhem Pasha had not, of course, arrived from Pharsala, where an action was taking place, and as Hakki had never contemplated taking Velestino by assault, which would have involved a needless loss of life, fighting was stopped for the day, and the arrival of Memdoukh's division and the advance of Hamdi on the right were awaited.

Velestino had, however, already been deserted, though of this the Turks were as yet unaware; but early next morning the advancing troops were only answered by a fire from the extreme heights of Pilaf Tépé, and on the cavalry pressing forward it was discovered that both the town and the third line of earthworks beyond it had been deserted. At the same time the Greeks above, though firing with their mountain guns, were occupied in dismounting the siege pieces which had been so laboriously dragged up some days before. Of this we knew nothing, and anticipating a final and more desperate stand from the almost impregnable position above, Hakki decided to delay a little longer until Hamdi had come into contact with the enemy.

In this way the whole of the 6th May and most of the 7th were wasted, and all that was done was that Hakki pushed forward his skirmishing lines, and drove the few remaining Greek troops of the right wing back on the batteries above. Memdoukh did not arrive until the afternoon of the 7th, having marched nearly all night, and his troops were then so tired that it was judged best to let them rest before attempting to turn or carry the position of Pilaf Tépé, which was still believed to be held; also it was then too late in the day to embark on any movement on a large scale. In the meantime Velestino had been occupied, and Edhem Pasha, who had arrived from Pharsala, had established his temporary headquarters in one of the houses, the outposts having been pushed forward half a mile beyond the town.

That night Weldon, Sonnenberg and myself bivouacked with an Albanian battalion, the colonel of which very kindly gave us a tent and some dried fish. We firmly expected to see a big battle next day, and had not as yet profited by our experience and guessed that the last of the Greeks had already decamped from their mountain top, and were even then embarking at Volo *en route* for Lamia and the main body at Domoko.

At dawn Memdoukh's division set out to the left on a long turning march, by which he was to pass the enemy's right and come down on Volo. Hardly had he started, however, when news came in from the outposts that a deputation from the Consular Corps had arrived from Volo to confer with the

XI THE SECOND BATTLE OF VELESTINO 87

Field-Marshal. At the same time the heights of Pilaf Tépé were reconnoitred and reported empty, and the vedettes accordingly moved slowly forward, meeting with no one except a few peasants.

Uncertain as to whether the entire force of the enemy had retreated on Volo, and wishing also to sweep the hills and disperse any irregular bands that might still be about, Edhem ordered Memdoukh to continue his march over the shoulders of Pelion, which he did, and descending into the plain of Volo next afternoon, returned to his original position at Velestino, whence he marched to Pharsala on the 9th.

All fighting being therefore over for the moment, nothing remains but to describe the interesting episode of the Consular deputation. On the 6th the Greek troops had come pouring in from Velestino and had at once commenced embarking on board their men-of-war lying in the harbour. A panic naturally then commenced among the civil population, and the Consuls of England and France and the Consular Agents of Austria, Russia, and Italy accordingly met together and decided to depute two of their number to go to meet Edhem Pasha and request his peaceable occupation of a defenceless town.

The two Consuls were selected by their colleagues, and they first visited the Greek Admiral, who would make no definite promise about not shelling the town, but gave them to understand that if no outrages or fires took place he would probably take no offensive action. Escorted by six bluejackets with flags from the British, French and Italian warships then lying in Volo Harbour, and accompanied by a few war correspondents, the Consuls next set out on their adventurous ride, or rather drive, about one in the morning of the 8th. All the Greek troops were then on board, and the town was convulsed with fear. Going very slowly in the dark the Consuls were challenged by the Turkish sentries about 3.30 a.m., and by very good luck not fired on. Their arrival was reported to Edhem Pasha, who received them an hour later. They then explained the state of affairs, and requested in the name of the town that the Turkish occupation should be peacefully effected, and that security of person and property should be insured. To this Edhem Pasha at once assented, and the deputation started back with one of the Imperial aide-de-camps, while some cavalry and two battalions were ordered to enter and take possession of Volo.

On getting there about nine o'clock we found the shops shut and the population somewhat excited, but otherwise the situation seemed normal. The Sultan's proclamation, in the sense of Edhem's guarantee, was immediately posted up on the walls of the town hall, and the mayor and municipal authorities were convened to discuss details with Enver Bey, who had been appointed military governor. The Greek flagship, the *Psara*, with the Admiral on board, still lay

XI THE SECOND BATTLE OF VELESTINO 89

out in the roadstead, and the Admiral was momentarily reported to be preparing to bombard the town. This was, however, on the face of it an extremely improbable event, and in point of fact he was merely waiting for orders from Athens to rejoin the rest of the fleet in Halmyros Bay. That evening he weighed anchor and steamed off, and the shipping of Volo was then only represented by a British and a French gunboat and an Italian ironclad. These three ships, a Turkish corporal informed me next day, had been captured from the Franks by the Ottoman fleet, which had now sailed away to "take Crete."

On the 8th, the day that Volo was occupied, patrols had been landed from the European ships to protect the Consulates, but at Edhem's request this duty was now taken over by the Turks. Everything remained very quiet, and there were no cases at all of burning or pillage, possibly due to the presence of international representatives and to the small number of troops that were in the town.

At Velestino the Turks had captured four guns and twenty cases of ammunition, and they now found two more guns and a quantity of war material and supplies of all sorts at Volo. Four other siege guns had also been sunk in the harbour by the Greeks, who had not had time enough to get them on board the fleet. There were, however, very few prisoners, such soldiers as had remained having exchanged their uniforms for the more secure garb of plain clothes. Besides these several ladies of the British Red Cross, two or three belated war correspondents, and the staff of the railway, were all that remained of the *personnel* of the Greek army. The latter had, however, effected two master strokes before its departure. It had cut all the telegraph wires leading anywhere, which materially hindered the transmission of news to Europe, though it did not particularly affect the convenience or movements of the Ottoman forces; and it had disembowelled all the locomotives, thereby raising the price of cabs to a premium. But a week later an adventurous Turkish officer of engineers discovered two homeless engines on the way to Trikkala, and a forgotten train somewhere near Pharsala. With the help of these he organised a railway service which ran once a day, and which was able to compete successfully with a mounted messenger.

The incident is quoted not so much for its practical value, which was small, as to prove that there really were engineers, the existence of such a corps having been frequently questioned and even denied by some of the Europeans present with the army.

CHAPTER XII

THE BATTLE OF DOMOKO

NORTHERN and Central Thessaly were now in the hands of the Turks, and it seemed that, unless a revolution occurred at Athens, the war must come to a speedy conclusion. The main body of the Greek army was concentrated at Domoko and a smaller force lay at Halmyros, supported by the fleet, while the Ottoman troops were massed at Pharsala, with the exception of the 5th Division, which still remained at Velestino. Edhem Pasha had therefore in his front line nearly 80,000 fighting men, while the Duke of Sparta commanded barely half that number. The Turks were in a fertile country, flushed by success and eager to go forward. On the other hand, their opponents had been driven into the barren mountain regions; they were disorganised and dispirited, and dissension was rife in every department of their army.

The change of feeling at Athens, consequent on the continued defeats, had affected the political situation, and the new Greek Cabinet under M. Ralli, after its first bellicose declarations, appeared anxious to accept the mediation which the Great Powers were still willing to undertake. It is not my intention to discuss the exchange of notes that went on between the Governments of the two belligerents and the representatives of the Powers during the ten days that elapsed between the taking of Volo and the battle of Domoko. The net result was that by May 17th no armistice had been actually signed, and it is not generally known whether or not Edhem Pasha had by then been notified of the Porte's intention to cease hostilities. It is, however, certain that had he advanced on Domoko a week earlier than he actually did, he could have inflicted a much more crushing blow on the Greeks, who were then neither ready nor fortified; but in the absence of diplomatic data one must forbear either to blame Edhem's strategy or to question the Porte's good faith.

On the morning of the 9th the headquarters staff, which had slept at Velestino, rode to Larissa, and next day proceeded thence to Tekke, a small village four miles north of Pharsala. Five divisions were now encamped in the plain, for Memdoukh and Hamdi had returned from Velestino, and Haidar had come up from the Milona Pass and Larissa. Some of the cavalry squadrons had obtained remounts from among the fresh packhorses coming in from the provinces, but the arm generally remained very weak, and was being continually drawn on for outside services.

THE BATTLE OF DOMOKO

On the 11th May a reconnaissance was made in the direction of Domoko, and some of the cavalry got close to the town. Beyond reporting that the enemy were there in force, and that they had fortified the heights, they brought back but little information. Edhem Pasha, however, now changed his tactics, and determined to employ a strong and prominent left wing in his next advance. Accordingly Hakki was directed to push forward from Velestino and dislodge the enemy's brigade in front of Halmyros. This he did, after a slight skirmish, in which Mr. Montgomery and Baron von Binder, the special correspondents of the *Standard* and the *Fremdemblatt* respectively, were taken prisoners by the Greeks and sent to Athens. The Greek land forces retired in the direction of Lamia, while the fleet, which had been hitherto cruising in the Gulf of Volo with its headquarters at Halmyros Bay, now retired to the Island of Skiatho and the mouth of the Atalanta Channel, continuing the blockade of the ports of Salonika and Volo on all shipping except warships of neutral powers.

On the 14th the troops from Metzovo belonging to the army of Janina advanced in order to establish connection with Islam Pasha at Trikkala, and Edhem was then appointed to the chief command of all the Imperial forces in Thessaly and Epirus.

In the meantime the commissariat arrangements at Pharsala were not by any means doing well. The presence of an immense number of men for ten or twelve days had begun to tell on the resources of the plain, and during the week before the battle of Domoko it was extremely hard to get food of the most simple kind. The Greeks appear to have been in no better case, for deserters were continually coming in to the Turkish camp with tales of the destitution and disorganisation that existed in the Hellenic lines; and it became manifest that a move must be made in some direction, or that the transport of supply must be accelerated and enlarged. Both the Turkish and the Red Crescent medical authorities had established field hospitals at Pharsala; and a Russian cruiser, the *Donetz*, arrived in Volo on the 13th with a detachment of the Red Cross, who at once proceeded to Pharsala, accompanied by an officer charged with a private mission to the Commander-in-Chief.

All these indications premised that, in spite of the negotiations that were known to be under discussion at Constantinople and Athens, some further fighting was contemplated, at any rate in the Turkish camp; and this idea was still further confirmed by the advance of the remaining brigade of Hakki Pasha's division to Halmyros, and the departure of Memdoukh's division in the same direction on the night of the 15th. The utmost secrecy, however, had been observed; and though the natural point of attack seemed to be Domoko, many expected a battle further to the east, while there were some who firmly believed that the Greek fleet, abandoning its passive *rôle*, was going to make a descent on Volo, to land troops and to cut the Turkish lines of communication. This diversion, though it could have no permanent success nor be of any material value, might create a temporary change of feeling in Europe, and the *éclat* of the recapture of Volo might obtain for the Hellenic Government better terms of peace than it could otherwise have cause to expect. As we know, however, no such move was made ; and the Greek Admiral, either in consequence of his orders or from his lack of initiative, was content to lie idle outside the Gulf of Volo, and to allow the war to finish without having struck one decisive blow, and without having in any way made effective use of the one arm in which the Greeks were supposed to excel their opponents.

On the night of the 15th Hakki concentrated his division in the advanced position of Halmyros, and Memdoukh formed the second step of the echelon by moving forward on his right rear. On the afternoon of the 16th far greater preparations were made, for the entire force at Pharsala paraded and prepared to advance. The general headquarters came forward from Tekke, the outposts were reinforced by a cavalry brigade, and every sign was given of an approaching engagement. About seven in the evening the troops began their march, and, going very slowly as the darkness came on, bivouacked at midnight within five or six miles of Domoko. No enemy had been met with, and the hill country through which we had passed seemed as deserted as it was silent. At first it had appeared as if Edhem Pasha intended delivering a night attack; but this idea was dispelled as soon as the divisions halted, and we understood that the fight was to be reserved for the morrow. The troops slept till dawn and then breakfasted, and soon after six recommenced their march. The order of the advance in column, which was also the line of battle, was as follows, viz. :—

On the extreme right was Hairi, with the First Division; he was somewhat in rear of the rest of the line and covered the corps artillery. Next on his left came Nechat (Second Division), his first brigade being armed with the new Mauser rifle; beyond him was Hamdi; and two miles in rear of the latter, for a reserve, was Haidar Pasha, who had had no fighting since the Battle of Milona. Five miles away Memdoukh was on the left front of Hamdi, and beyond him again Hakki formed the most advanced and southern face of the echelon. The idea of the battle then was to drive the Greeks away from their base at Lamia, and to cut off effectively their line of retreat from Domoko. Neither of these objects were attained, and though the Greeks by the most inexcusable blunders relinquished an almost impregnable position and omitted to hold another vital point behind, yet the Turks practically obtained the minimum amount of success, and what they did obtain simply by courage and weight of numbers.

THE BATTLE OF DOMOKO

As we emerged from the hills that fringe its northern edge, the plain of Domoko with its rocky citadel burst upon our view. The scene was so remarkable and so typical of Greece that it merits some fuller description.

Beyond a broad valley some ten miles long and five broad, dotted with a few cornfields, but for the most part covered with wild grass, rose a frowning height. The face of this rock was traversed by a succession of natural terraces rising one above the other and marking the ascent of the winding road that led to the summit, where stood the town and fortress of Domoko, perched up aloft and dominating from its crags the entire plain below.

Four miles to the left the valley ended in a cul de sac, the northern and southern hills meeting one another in a narrow gorge: to the right the country gradually widened out until a lower chain of mountains lifted the eye to the mighty Pindus range beyond.

The interest of the landscape was however almost entirely eclipsed by the contemplation of what was probably one of the strongest defensive positions ever selected by a general. At the foot of the opposite cliff lay three or four lines of infantry intrenched, only to be descried by the artificial straightness of their earthworks. Beyond these some dense black masses marked their reserves, while behind and above each terrace bristled with cannon, their muzzles peeping through the embrasures, until on the very crest four great siege guns crowned the ramparts of the citadel, completing the defence.

On debouching into the plain Hamdi at once moved off to the left, and began to scale the hills at the eastern end of the valley; by ten o'clock we had lost sight of him, but we could hear the sound of his infantry firing all day, and sometimes could even distinguish the cannonade of Memdoukh far away to his left. Hamdi performed a long and wearisome flank march, and had comparatively little fighting, but it was almost entirely due to his patient advance that one day terminated the battle, and that both sides were spared the immense loss of life that would inevitably have accompanied an assault.

At the same time that Hamdi commenced his march to the left Hairi moved in a diagonal direction half-right, and after proceeding about three miles halted and piled arms behind a broad low mamelon that lay a mile and a half from the foot of the Domoko cliff.

Haidar Pasha and Riza with the head of the corps artillery, remained at the entrance to the plain, so that on the Second Division devolved the main attack, and, as will be seen, the real brunt of the battle. A few shots were fired about midday by a line of two of its battalions extended in skirmishing order, and the most forward Greek outposts at once fell back on the first intrenchments, and a pause of nearly two hours ensued. This was to allow the divisions on the left to make good their advance and to preserve the echelon of the army.

At 2 P.M. the first (Islam Pasha's) brigade of Nechat's division, which had been halted a mile from the enemy, deployed and commenced to advance. Firing, which had been carried on for some time on the left, now at once commenced in earnest, and the brigade (six battalions in line of quarter columns) changed its formation to line.

The Greek artillery, which had evidently studied and learnt the range, poured in shrapnel during the execution of this movement with disastrous effect. Nechat then sent two batteries forward, and they proceeded to shell the trenches, but it was impossible to see with what result.

Hairi on the right advanced a single battery, which fired about a dozen shots and then relapsed into silence. No attempt, however, was made to bring up the corps artillery. In consequence Islam was practically unsupported, and had to continue his attack over level ground varied by occasional corn fields, in the teeth of a most murderous shrapnel fire from an almost invisible enemy.

This advance went on for about an hour and a half, during which the 5,000 men composing the attacking force lost nearly one fifth of their numbers killed or wounded. It was the most inhuman spectacle imaginable, as the men could be seen dropping right and left, while the masses of their comrades of the 1st Division remained in rear protected by the ground and apparently without any intention of going to their support.

The forward movement was necessarily of the slowest, and in the ninety odd minutes that it lasted barely 1,000 yards were gained. The firing throughout was furious, and, though the losses on both sides were very heavy, the expenditure of ammunition was as usual out of proportion to the casualties. At no moment, however, could one notice the least sign of wavering in the Turkish line, and the men engaged appeared to regard the whole thing as a pleasure excursion in which they had the good fortune to be in front.

At half-past four the fire slackened very noticeably, as both sides were beginning to run out of ammunition; and then, and only then, did Nechat deploy the second brigade of his division. At the same time the long expected batteries of the corps artillery could be seen approaching across the plain.

The second brigade came up comparatively rapidly, and the Greeks committed the unpardonable error of allowing it to advance without firing on it. By five o'clock it had arrived in line with the first brigade, and almost at the same moment the bursting of a Greek gun on the mountain side was signalised by a tall spirt of flame. The enemy then began to retire from the first line of intrenchments, and the Turks, 500 yards off, did not delay to follow them up.

The tables were now turned. The Greek ammunition was nearly spent, the Turks had just

THE ROAD TO THE SOUTH.

[*To face p.* 101.

received a fresh supply. A rattling musketry fire was poured into the enemy's back, doing wide execution, and by half-past five Riza Pasha's leading batteries came into action alongside of Nechat's guns and began to rake the opposite slopes with shell and shrapnel. The Greek artillery replied in kind, and for a time no effort was relaxed by the gunners on either side. But it was obvious that, however much the retiring infantry might lose for the moment, directly they had all reached the shelter of the slopes, where the second line was intrenched, the effect of the Turkish fire on the protected guns of the Greeks would be comparatively small. The event seemed uncertain, and it remained for Hamdi to decide it.

Few of the spectators had paid much attention to his advance, which was only distinguishable by ear; and now, when at six o'clock his leading companies appeared on the hills near the Greek right flank, few realised who and what they were. Their identity, however, did not long remain doubtful, for in ten minutes a battery was in action and a sharp infantry fire was also enfilading the lower lines of the Greek guns. As his men poured over the summit of the hills the issue of the battle became clear. The enemy's guns in the lower terraces ceased firing, and their infantry began to mount still higher up the slopes. But it was getting late and also getting dark; the only troops available to push the defeat home were already tired out, and some battalions were decimated twice over. Also Edhem Pasha, who was now with the artillery, rightly judged that a night's rest might in all ways produce as good net results for the Ottoman arms as a night attack. At eight o'clock, therefore, firing was ceased, bivouac fires were lighted by the Turks in the Greek earthworks, and only a dropping cannonade far away to the east marked Memdoukh's distant advance.

At dawn every one was on the move, but no shot sounded from the Greek lines, and as the Turkish infantry advanced it entered only empty trenches. The enemy, fearing to see their line of retreat cut, and unwilling to risk any further loss, had fled in the night, leaving their big guns, much of their ammunition, and such baggage as they still possessed. On the whole there is no doubt that they had followed the wisest course. For as they had not protected either their flank or their rear, when both were threatened they had to elect between annihilation and retreat. It is no slur on their courage that they chose the latter.

CHAPTER XIII

THE OCCUPATION OF SOUTHERN THESSALY

FORTUNATELY for the Greeks neither Hakki nor Memdoukh had pushed sufficiently forward to enable them to effectively cut the line of retreat on Lamia. The reason of this was that the country over which they had to march was extremely mountainous and intersected by steep narrow ravines. It was necessary to keep their artillery with them, as they might meet with the entire force of the Hellenic army, and to do this they had to make long and tedious circuits. The consequence was that only Memdoukh's advanced skirmishers came into contact with the enemy, who marched rapidly along the only road, and the Turks were thus unable to come to really close quarters or to inflict any permanent damage; also their approach hastened the Greek flight.

What advantage was taken of the Domoko victory was entirely due to the initiative of Hamdi and Sefulat Pashas. Hamdi, as we know, had occupied the lower hills to the east of Domoko on the evening of the 17th, and was there much nearer to the road than any of the other Turkish troops. Sefulat, who was now chief of the General Staff, quickly saw this, and immediately came to the 6th Division and urged Hamdi to take up the pursuit, it being at that time difficult to communicate with Edhem, who was some miles away. It was, however, impossible for Hamdi to advance at once, as his troops were tired out, and had barely eaten for twenty-four hours. But he ordered four battalions to commence the march at 6 A.M., and lent Sefulat his cavalry (one squadron) and one battery. Sefulat had also collected two more squadrons on his way to Hamdi, and with this force he prepared to follow up the entire Greek army.

Starting at dawn on the 18th he pushed on with all speed, and by midday had arrived at the foot of the Phurka Pass, where the main Othrys range marks the southern boundary of Thessaly. The enemy had halted in some force on the heights, and a considerable amount of time was wasted in endeavouring to discover how strong they were. As it happened, they did not utilise this interval to construct any intrenchments, being indeed only a weak rearguard, and having halted more to reform and collect stragglers than to make any permanent resistance

By three o'clock the four battalions from Hamdi's division began to come up, and Sefulat then ad-

XIII THE OCCUPATION OF SOUTHERN THESSALY

vanced, making a great show with his battery, and dismounting his cavalry to assist in the attack.

At five o'clock, as the troops got well up the pass, slight firing commenced from the enemy above, but a few well-directed shots from the Turkish artillery in the plain and a rattling fusillade from the infantry soon caused them to relinquish their position, and, after an engagement that lasted barely an hour, they retired down the slopes on the southern side of the pass and left the col free. The Turks immediately mounted and occupied the crest in force; but darkness was already falling, and the men were also very tired, so Sefulat decided to halt there for the night. He had done all that was necessary; it was quite impossible with so few troops to pursue and cut up the retreating Greeks, whereas the possession of the pass, the last good defensible position on the road to the south, was of the utmost value. It was believed that the mass of the Greek army would make some stand in the plain of Lamia, where they were based on the fleet which lay in the bay, and where they had behind them Thermopylæ, whose name, at any rate, might encourage them, though its natural strength was not by any means very great.

The Turks spent the night on the Phurka Pass; and early next morning, the 19th, the rest of Hamdi's division, with two extra batteries from the corps artillery, arrived, and began to cross the mountains. The road is not difficult, and by midday the entire force was well in the plain, and, advancing towards the sea, found the Greeks drawn up in battle array some two miles to the north of Lamia. Nearly an hour before this, the skirmishers and cavalry that Sefulat had thrown forward had come into action, but the firing was only desultory.

The Greeks were estimated at not more than 10,000 strong, and they had only two batteries with them, so that it was obvious that no long stand could be made unless they received reinforcements.

Their line lay along a low ridge of hills, and the infantry on both sides began firing at a distance of over 1,000 yards. The Greek artillery was not engaged, though the Turkish guns came into action. Rumours had now become general of an armistice, though as yet no one appeared to have any certain information. A deputation had come headed by the Mayor of Lamia, asking for the peaceable occupation of the town, which lay outside the actual field of operations, the main road to the south skirting it well on the right. Sefulat replied that he was unable to treat while the Greek forces lay between him and the city, but that if no resistance was made the civil population need fear nothing. The Mayor therefore went back about ten o'clock, and by 1 P.M. the conflict had become general.

An hour later the fire slackened considerably on the Greek side, and almost at once a large white flag was hoisted in their lines, and the "cease firing" was loudly blown.

XIII THE OCCUPATION OF SOUTHERN THESSALY

After a little delay the Turkish bugles also sounded, and in a few minutes two Greek staff officers, accompanied by a trumpeter and a flag of truce, were seen to be advancing towards us. They were received by Sefulat Pasha, and a short conversation took place, after which the Greek officers rode back to their lines. No more firing took place, and the Greek troops soon began to move off in the direction of Thermopylae, leaving Lamia on their left, and by five o'clock were quite out of sight beyond the hills.

The Turks, however, did not advance, nor was Lamia occupied, and it was then understood that Sefulat had agreed to a cessation of hostilities for twenty-four hours, during which the Turks undertook not to advance.

This news was at once communicated to Edhem Pasha, who had remained at Domoko, and had now received his orders from Constantinople; and next day at one o'clock in the afternoon, before the expiration of the truce, a further mission arrived from the Crown Prince's head-quarters, and an armistice for fifteen days was signed by the representatives of both armies.

The same day a similar armistice had been signed on the bridge at Arta by the respective commanders; and on June 3rd a further arrangement was made by which all offensive operations were to be suspended during the progress of the peace negotiations, *i.e.* for an indefinite period. This, however, was terminable by either party at twenty-four hours' notice.

On May 20th, the foreign military attachés and the war correspondents took leave of the Commander-in-Chief at Domoko, and he then proceeded with his staff to meet the officers deputed by the Crown Prince, and with them to lay down the neutral zone some 1,000 yards broad, into which the forces of neither army were to pass.

On May 21st, Lamia was occupied by a few Turkish troops, but they were soon withdrawn under the conditions of the armistice. Up to date there have been several further reports of infractions of the armistice, but of the truth of these I am unable to speak, and they are probably events of small importance.

The general situation in Thessaly was therefore as follows:—The Turkish forces lay along the ancient frontier except in the western Greek nomarchy, where the Hellenic army still held Arta. In Epirus, the events, very briefly summed up, had been that the Greeks under Colonel Manos had advanced up country as far as Pentepigadia, but after a few ephemeral successes they had been driven back to their starting point. Prevesa, a Turkish fort at the entrance to the Ambracian Gulf, had been bombarded for some days by the Greek fleet, but had not succumbed, and to all intents and purposes the position on the Ionian coast was very much the same as it had been previous to the declaration of war.

XIII THE OCCUPATION OF SOUTHERN THESSALY

In Thessaly headquarters remained for the time being at Domoko, and a field hospital was established there, as the last Turkish losses had been very severe. Indeed, the battle field the day after the fight was a really pitiful sight, being covered with corpses of men and horses, conspicuous amongst the enemy's dead being the Garibaldians with their red shirts. It is calculated that between three and four hundred Turks were killed at Domoko, and there were twice that number of wounded.

Throughout the campaign, however, it was the most difficult thing in the world to get statistics of the casualties. It is doubtful whether any lists were kept, and even if they were they were probably incomplete, and would have been unreliable if communicated officially. Personally I believe that the total Turkish loss in dead was not much over 1,500, and the ordinary proportion of battles would give double that number of wounded. Therefore altogether, including the sick, who were few, it may be assumed that 5,000 represents the total number of men in the Ottoman army placed *hors de combat* during the war.

As has been said then, the Turks had occupied the whole of Thessaly, the line held by their armies being practically shown by the course of latitude 39°. Most of their troops lay to the front, but the 4th Division still remained at Pharsala, and the 7th at Larissa. Islam Pasha's command, which for the sake of identity I have marked in the maps as the

9th Division, although it was never styled so, lay at Trikkala, and the communication between the armies of the east and west had been effected by the advance of a force from Metzovo, which now lay between Domoko and Arta. In the meantime, the 8th, or Konieh Division, which had been slowly coming over from Asia Minor by way of Rodosto, Salonika, and Sorovitch, had begun to arrive at Elassona, and by the 25th of May was concentrated at that place. The men, like the 7th Division, were armed with the Mauser rifle and were nearly all Redifs. We passed them on our way back to Salonika, and were especially struck by their hardy fit appearance and their pleasant manner. They looked every inch good fighting men.

The country at that time, the end of May, seemed almost in its normal state again. Many of the Greeks had returned to their ordinary avocations, most of the shops were open in the towns, and some of the corn was being cut in the fields. Macedonia was still more quiet, the peasants there being fully occupied with the transport of baggage and provisions for the advancing reinforcements. Since then there have been fresh mobilisations in Asia Minor and fresh movements of troops to the front. Also there have been reports of depredations by the Ottoman irregulars in Thessaly. As there are now few correspondents there, it is difficult to verify these statements, which all, of course, emanate from Greek sources. But while we were in Thessaly,

XIII THE OCCUPATION OF SOUTHERN THESSALY

beyond the occasional burning of a house, probably more due to carelessness than anything else, and the casual appropriation of a few sheep, there was hardly any pillage, and to my knowledge no outrage. It is of course wrong to burn an empty house or to steal a lamb; but it must be remembered that the perpetrators of these crimes were wholly uneducated men from the wilds of Asia Minor, who were under the impression that they were obeying their sovereign's orders, and who were undoubtedly in the exercise of the ordinary rights of war.

It is perhaps fair therefore not to be too hard on the Turks, and to remember that reports from purely Greek sources require to be authenticated before being unhesitatingly believed.

On the other hand, even according to their own newspapers, the condition of the province of Phocis, where the Greek army took up its quarters after the armistice, is anything but secure. Bands of irregulars and itinerant parties of marauders appear to be as numerous as the King's forces, and probably real pillage is much more common there than it is on the Turkish side of the zone. Outrage has not existed, or had not when I was there; and although Edhem Pasha has been endowed by the Sultan with the title of "Ghazi," which means a "religious conqueror," the war was at no time a religious war; indeed, on the Ottoman side it was hardly national. For both officers and men looked upon it more as a game than anything else; and though intrigue may now give its results a false direction, in its execution it was purely a punitive enforcement of diplomacy.

CHAPTER XIV

CONCLUSION

HAVING headed one's first chapter "The Causes of the War," it seems in the fitness of things to end with the "War's Results." But as yet the results can hardly be known to the directors of the foreign policies of Europe. Nothing remains, therefore, but to give the general impressions produced by the campaign and its incidents on one who followed it more from its soldiering than its diplomatic side, and who was somewhat handicapped by being that most suspicious of all things to the Oriental mind, a newspaper correspondent. Having already dwelt rather lengthily on military details, a brief summary of matters connected with the armies will probably suffice the civilian reader. These can best be dealt with under the heads of strategy, tactics, the three arms, the non-combatant services, and general organisation. Beyond this a brief glance at what were really far more interesting, the national and individual characteristics of the men and their officers, will bring this record to an end. But there is no doubt that if all the intrigues and inner history of the war were known, they would afford a far more interesting study to the student of the Turk and the Greek than the most careful consideration of their respective warlike operations. For Oriental diplomacy, if it can be so called, is at any rate instructive in its devious courses.

The strategy of the Turks was essentially dilatory; but, though apparently always over cautious, they failed to show a just appreciation of the real dangers of war. They entirely ignored the true object of attack, the enemy's base, and advanced with a strong right instead of a strong left wing. They omitted to push home their advantages, and even the little cavalry they had was rarely employed. Immensely strong in artillery, they hardly ever made use of this arm in great masses; and, having only to fear one thing, a cutting of their lines of communication, they left these during the first part of the campaign almost unprotected and in no way organised. On the other hand, they never made rash movements, they always concentrated a force superior to the enemy's before giving battle (except in Mahmud's case), and they evidently understood, though they did not always apply, the lessons taught by the Russo-Turkish war as regards the thousand and one non-combatant services which go to make up the backbone of an army.

The Greek strategy was on the whole reasonable—their main object, having declared war, was to gain time, and this they certainly managed to do, though more because of their enemy's halting advance than from any other cause. Their commissariat and supply arrangements were wretched, but this was simply because they had no material, not because they did not understand its necessity. In medical assistance they relied on Europe, and were not disappointed. By a succession of extraordinary tactics they invariably had to desert almost impregnable positions, but they always fell back on their base and their ships. Whether they were right in dividing their small forces is doubtful: probably they were; for points like Trikkala and Larissa, Pharsala and Velestino, were equally dangerous in the enemy's hands; but there is no doubt that they erred in the most deplorable manner in allowing their fleet to remain practically useless during the whole war, and to select for its ineffective attack the one place where it was unlikely to obtain any striking success, Prevesa.

We now come to the region of tactics. The Turks' tactics, as far as they had any, were to bang away at the enemy till they beat him—an excellent idea when you have enough men, and in their case very successful. On one or two occasions some elementary movements, such as flank attacks, and once an envelopment, were evolved from the commanders' brains, but they never got much further and had little result to show. At the battle of Domoko had any but the Hellenic army been defending the position, Hamdi Pasha would never have scaled the hills; as it was his advance passed for a triumph of tactical skill, rather than for a very heroic and plodding fighting march, which is what it really was.

If, however, the Turks were deficient in this branch of the ethics of war the Greeks were many degrees below them. It is unfair to generalise from isolated incidents; but one or two examples of their stupendous want of foresight to some extent indicate the main method of procedure. At Tyrnavos they left the telegraph line uncut; at Larissa, Pharsala, and Domoko they deserted masses of Krupp ammunition; at Velestino they dragged some great siege guns up to a commanding height, kept them there two days during a battle, never fired a shot from them, and then with infinite labour dragged them down only to sink them in the Gulf of Volo. They generally omitted to protect their flanks, they only once detailed a rearguard, and in no case did they ever attempt to retard the Turkish advance by the simple expedients of blowing up a bridge or erecting any kind of obstacle.

It is a thankless task to find fault, though not very difficult; and I can only adduce as my excuse that these opinions were supported by most of the European officers present, and that it is necessary to draw attention to the peculiar absence of tactical knowledge in both armies in order to do proper justice to the wonderful courage of the men. Of

TURKISH FIELD BATTERY IN ACTION.

[To face p. 117.

the three arms on both sides the artillery obtained the best results, the Greek fire being on the whole more destructive than that of the Turks. Among the latter, battery commanders had as a rule had some technical instruction, commanders of guns none. Shrapnel was often employed when shell would have done, and *vice versa;* and the drill, speed and manœuvring were distinctly poor. The horses were kept in good order, and the supply of ammunition was as a rule up to the mark. The ranges were frequently misjudged towards the beginning of the war; but latterly, especially on the Greek side, battery commanders evinced more aptitude than before. Firing was often begun when the enemy was too far off, and the effects of indirect fire were always poor among the Turks. The proportion of shell to bullet wounds was large, and this to some extent bore out the better aiming of the Greek gunners.

The Greek cavalry I only saw once, and cannot therefore give an opinion of much value about it. It was said to consist of twelve squadrons, and the riding was reported as bad. Its best known exploit was the capture at Halmyros of two war correspondents. It seems to have been ill-disciplined, as the men threw away many of their heavier accoutrements at both Larissa and Pharsala.

The Turkish cavalry was the most excellent material, well mounted, fairly led, and badly drilled. What they lacked in training, however, they made up in valour; and had they only been a little more numerous, and given a few more opportunities, they would no doubt have distinguished themselves considerably. The men were well dressed and the horses well cared for, though sometimes rather too fat. Squadron leaders were slow in the field, but the interior economy was good. Divisional cavalry was rarely employed, except in outside duties, and the commander of the cavalry division was not a Blucher. The remount arrangements were *nil*.

The chief arm was of course the infantry. Of the Turks the pure Osmanlis were distinctly the best soldiers, and the Albanians, as a whole, belied their reputation. They are not particularly amenable to discipline, and it is just conceivable that they might turn back if heavily pressed. On the other hand, the Turk, unless ordered, is incapable of running away, and when he has got an order he will observe it, *ruat cœlum*. His courage and his calm and silent advance beggar description, and there is little doubt that when the Turkish army is really trained up to a high European standard it will be invincible. At present the shooting and the fire discipline are poor, not because the men do not obey, but because the officers do not command. A Turkish captain would as soon think of adjusting his men's sights, or of ordering them to cease independent firing, as he would of reading a book on military history.

The deployments, &c., were imperfect, and the

advance by rushes did not exist; nevertheless, there are few more inspiring sights than an attack of Turkish troops.

As regards the Greek infantry, it is hard to come to a conclusion. Courage they certainly had, but only of a particular—the defensive—kind. Behind intrenchments they were excellent, but when it became a question of charging they appeared to lose their nerve. Their shooting and drill, if a little more superficial, was not really much better than that of the Turks. Their officers were by no means good, and their discipline was at no time reliable. Even the exceptional case of the flight from Tyrnavos must speak volumes. No Turkish force could be driven to such a moral extremity.

The Euzonoi, light troops and mountaineers, were the best of the Greek army. The rest were for the most part townsmen and labourers, who had no idea that they were undertaking anything more than a triumphal march to Salonika. When they discovered their mistake some of them deserted; but the majority did their best to acquire in a short time the rudiments of a calling which was not their own, and for which they had no special aptitude.

The Italian volunteers I believe gave more trouble than they were worth; and the lack of organisation in the Foreign Legion tended generally to impair its fighting value. Its courage was, however, beyond dispute, and it probably included the most honest and most fervid Phil-hellenes in the whole army.

Of the non-combatant services I have already spoken in various places. Transport was good in the Turkish army, so was ammunition supply, as a rule. Engineers and technical arms, such as ballooning, heliographing, &c., were practically non-existent. Field-telegraph was reasonably quick, though under-officered. Postal service south of Elassona very slow and intermittent. Railway arrangements on the Monastir line good (under Austrian control); on the Larissa line very backward, and very long in getting under way. Staff work not up to the mark—orderlies much quicker than aides-de-camp—orders hardly ever written. Medical corps and transport of wounded fair but not remarkable (I am not of course alluding here to the Red Crescent). Censorship of the press erratic but not bigoted. The above are the main items.

Of the corresponding services on the Greek side, the field train as a whole was sadly deficient, but the supply of ammunition in action was fairly well maintained. Transport of food, while in the plain and the bigger towns, was good; latterly, when everything became demoralised, very poor indeed. Technical arms good in theory, but lacking in *personnel*. Telegraph service bad, generally consisting of only a single line, and this often entirely appropriated to the headquarters staff. Postal service at first spasmodic, latterly non-existent. Railway service good (Russian management). Staff work, quick and efficient. Hospitals, &c., quite incompetent—but this service was discharged by detachments of the Red Cross, who worked efficiently and generously throughout. Transport of wounded (left to the army authorities), very bad. Censorship of the press quite remarkable. As I am informed by my colleagues on the Greek side, press telegrams, containing news in no way relating to military movements, and not even remarks detrimental to Greek prestige in general, were frequently not only tampered with or stopped without the senders being informed, but in several cases were absolutely altered and despatched to the European capitals containing a quite garbled version of the truth. No facilities for telegraphing were latterly given to correspondents, and the methods in which the examination and despatch of telegrams was conducted by the military and political authorities at headquarters and Athens were as extraordinary as they were unsound.

As to the question of organisation, the mobilisation schemes of both armies on paper were, of course, excellent. The Turks carried through theirs for the most part, but on the Greek side nearly all the plans broke down.

In the Ottoman army the concentration of troops, the transport of material to the front, and the purchase, despatch, and supply of pack animals was quite worthy of any European army, not excluding the German. As the campaign wore on, and there seemed to be no pressing needs, there was a noticeable slackness, especially on the lines of communication. But generally speaking, the total result was good, and should certainly have astonished the most sanguine of Turkey's military critics. On the Greek side everything was rather lamentable, and it was evident that the spirit of order had not as yet implanted itself in the Hellenic mind. The army was fairly quickly brought together, but nearly all other details were neglected, and the most that can be said in mitigation of the general *débacle* was that it was not wholly unexpected.

That the war was protracted as long as it was was due mainly to the slowness of the Turkish advance and to the pluck of a few of the Greek commanders, notably Smolenski.

The conclusion then, from a military point of view, was as follows: neither army was in reality mobile, but the Turks showed themselves distinctly capable of mobility. They are, to start with, good fighters, they are very enduring, they have immense marching powers, they carry nothing but their rifle, ammunition, and water-bottle (at a pinch they will dispense with this last), they are contented with the hardest life, they neither need nor want stimulants nor pleasure, and they enjoy battle. Add to this, if you can, really brave, capable and acceptable officers, increase the organisation to the utmost pitch of proficiency (this is merely a mechanical matter—*vide* the progress of the Russians)—impart a thorough moral and physical training to all ranks, and you will have the most exceptionally strong army that has ever been let loose on the earth. When the next Alexander or the next Napoleon arises he will find this out, and he will lead either the Chinese or the Turks. If he does so, he will obtain all that his ambition may desire, and the world can only pray that he may be sufficiently civilised not to desire wholesale devastation.

There are in the Balkan Peninsula three influences at work, none as yet very strong. The first is Panhellenism, rather superficial and extraneous and not very sound. The second is Panislamism, not by any means effete, and latterly greatly invigorated, but of too despotic a tendency and too passive a nature to obtain big results nowadays. The third is Panslavism, quiet and absorbing, and not as yet much seen, but comprehensive in scope and diplomatic in action. This is the little cloud; and it would be well to prevent the union of Behemoth with Leviathan while there is time.

Life on the whole was very pleasant during the campaign: there were no luxuries and very few comforts, but the Turkish officers were hospitable and agreeable, and far better informed on ordinary topics than is generally believed. I had travelled before in Armenia, so I knew some of them, and introductions are easily effected. You meet a man who has a brother whose friend you heard of in

Erzerum two years ago. That is sufficient excuse for the man to come and call on you at six o'clock next morning with four of his friends and to remain three hours. Needless to say there was always as much society as one desired. The Young Turkish Party was well represented; but at present it seems to be more talk than anything else, at any rate in Turkey. It has, however, a thorough appreciation of the benefits of a pure administration, a full exchequer, and a good education; unfortunately, when offered a pashalic, the most rabid reformer generally reverts to the ideas of his ancestors. When he gets the chance, however, he governs wisely, as a rule, and tries to be honest, which is a beginning. The old Turk, on the other hand, is disappearing; he feels behindhand whether in war or in peace, so he shuts himself up in his serai, and his children belong to the new generation.

There are two things to which I have not alluded —one is the incident of Osman Pasha and the other the German influence during the war.

Osman was sent out from Constantinople towards the end of April to take over the command-in-chief. Just as he was leaving Salonika he was recalled. The whole history of this turned on a Palace intrigue, which bears so slightly on the campaign, and which affected its course so little, that it has seemed best to leave it alone: the affair is probably already forgotten everywhere except at Yildiz, and may therefore repose in the oblivion it deserves.

The other thing, the German influence, is more important, not so much from the military results it produced as from the way it shows the general tendency of thought and attraction in the Ottoman Empire at the present time.

The army had, to a great extent, been organised on the German system, and some Prussian officers had held positions of control and direction on the general staff. The only German officer in the Turkish service who was with the army was Grumbkov Pasha, Inspector-General of Artillery: he remained six days, and though he did actually take Larissa, it was prepared for him and was not a very great exploit. On the other hand, there was a German military attaché and no less than six war correspondents, all of whom were or had been officers in the German army. There was no Russian or British military attaché, and Captain von Morgen accordingly came in for a good deal of Edhem Pasha's confidence. To what extent the Commander-in-Chief took his advice it is impossible to say. But the main point was the undeniable advance that German prestige has made in Turkey during the last two years. In 1895 and 1896 I was in Asia Minor, and then the words "Ingiliz" or "Russ" comprehended the average peasant's whole idea of the nations of Europe. Now it is quite different. Every one knows what "Allemán" means—it is the friend of Turkey, the country of the great Padishah of Firengistan, the place that sends the good cheap wares to Turkey. I remember once riding in to Larissa late at night with a Circassian trooper as escort, and as we came to the gate in the dark we were challenged. "Who goes there?" cried the sentry. "Allemán Pashá," gratuitously yelled out my man. As I did not know the parole I decided to leave the Pasha part of it alone till I got inside, but I called out, "Ben Ingilizim" (I am English). The gate was opened and we rode in and found the guard turned out. I asked the lieutenant why, expecting that the five brevets conferred on me by my trooper were the reason. Not a bit of it. "Effendim," he said, "I turned out the guard because I thought you were German."

As a matter of fact, the whole war was very considerably utilised by the Germans to push forward their commerce; and to a great extent they stepped into the places evacuated by the Greek traders in Constantinople and the Levant. Several of the railways are already in the hands of German companies, and the army will probably now become more German than ever; so that unless some opposition is made, we may really lose what foothold, political or commercial, we still have in Turkey.

* * * * * * * *

There remains little more to say. On the evening of May 22nd, as there appeared no likelihood of a steamer putting into Volo for some days, I started off for Larissa with Captain Ryder, who had come out before the battle of Domoko, Weldon and Sonnenburg deciding to remain at Volo a little longer. We drove all night, and getting to Larissa early in the morning, pushed on the same evening to Elassona. There we got a new carriage, and drove by Serfije and Cojani to Sorovitch, where we caught the train to Salonika. The weather was extremely hot and the country seemed quiet, and in some places the corn was being cut. Many of the Albanian volunteers were going back home, but they were far outnumbered by the fresh regular troops that were pouring along to the front. To a great extent the peasants were occupied with transport, but in the towns the people were following their ordinary business. I stayed a night in Salonika, to say good-bye to Mr. Blunt and my other friends, and caught the Orient Express at Nisch next evening. Three days afterwards, on May 29th, I arrived in London, after a very interesting ten weeks' excursion.

APPENDIX

SYNOPSIS OF EVENTS

Feb.	15.	Colonel Vassos lands in Crete.
March	1.	Turks and Greeks concentrate troops in Macedonia, Epirus and Thessaly.
,,	15.	Headquarters Turkish armies fixed at Elassona and Janina. Greek headquarters at Larissa and Arta.
April	1.	Six Turkish divisions in Macedonia, two in Epirus. Four Greek divisions in all Thessaly.
,,	8.	Raid of Grevena.
,, ,,	13. 14. }	Incidents at Shuma.
,,	16.	Incursion at Karya.
,,	17.	Declaration of war. Greeks advance from Arta.
,,	18.	Battle of Milona. Fighting at Skumpa, Damasi and Karya.
,, ,,	20. 21. }	Bombardment of Kritiri.
,,	21.	Battle of Mati. Fighting at Rapsani.
,,	23.	Bombardment of Katerina. Greeks advance on Pentepigadia.
,,	24.	Capture of Tyrnavos. Advance of 6th Division.
,,	25.	Capture of Larissa.
,,	27.	Capture of Zarkos.

APPENDIX

April 29. Capture of Trikkala. Greeks retire on Arta.
" 30. First battle of Velestino. Turks retire on Gherli.
May 1. Reinforcements to Gherli.
" 3. Capture of Karditsa.
" 4. 7th Division arrives at Elassona. 9th Division advances from Diskata.
" 5. Action at Pharsala. Second battle of Velestino.
" 6. Capture of Pharsala and Velestino.
" 7. Turks advance on Arta.
" 8. Capitulation of Volo.
" 11. Action of Halmyros.
" 14. Edhem Pasha in command of Turkish forces in Thessaly and Epirus. Turks advance from Metzovo.
" 15. Capture of Halmyros.
" 17. Battle of Domoko.
" 18. Capture of Domoko. Action at Phurka Pass. Connection established between Turkish armies of east and west. Truce made at Arta.
" 19. Action of Lamia. Truce made near Lamia.
" 20. Armistice signed in Thessaly and Epirus.
" 24. 8th Division arrives at Elassona.
June 3. Armistice prolonged during peace negotiations.

THE END

www.ingramcontent.com/pod-product-compliance
Lightning Source LLC
Chambersburg PA
CBHW031254230426
43670CB00005B/180